the
GREEN
website
guide

for better living

DEBORAH GRAY

southbank
publishing

First published in 2008 by Southbank Publishing,
21 Great Ormond Street, London WC1N 3JB

www.southbankpublishing.com

A CIP catalogue record for this book is available from the British Library.

ISBN 978-1-904915-33-1

2 4 6 8 10 9 7 5 3 1

Typeset by Avocet Typeset, Chilton, Aylesbury, Bucks
Printed and bound in Great Britain by CPD, Blaina, Wales

The Green Website Guide...

Contents

Introduction

In writing *The Green Website Guide* I have come to appreciate the vastness of the internet as a resource for the environmentalist or those who are simply concerned about the welfare of the planet. It has been hard to stay focused and not become overwhelmed by the scale and complexity of the issues as presented in this virtual library. The global crisis facing us in terms of biodiversity and climate change is undeniable, but it isn't all doom and gloom. Taking each issue individually, there is an amazing amount of work being done both at home and abroad to try to make a difference. This can be seen time and time again on sites run by charities, academics and committed individuals, all of whom are playing their part to make the world a better place in which to live. However, the worry is that all this is too little too late, and that well-intentioned words are not translated into global action. This is true for each one of us as individuals (putting our money where our mouth is), at a corporate level (for instance, supermarkets are making admirable green promises) and particularly at government level (much of the material on government sites is hugely encouraging).

Unlike conventional books, *The Green Website Guide* provides the reader with the opportunity to pick and mix, investigating topics on an ad hoc basis and from a number of different perspectives. The suggested sites within each section are loaded with ideas on how we – as individuals, collectively in our communities and as nations – can move the agenda forward and make real change. It won't be an easy ride and it is clear that those of us that lead privileged western lifestyles are going to have to make some painful sacrifices. In their 'One Planet Living' campaign (**www.wwf. org.uk/core/takeaction/rethink.asp**), the World Wildlife Fund provide a clear but extensive summary of the small steps we can all take to make a difference. They point out that in the UK we are currently living beyond our means and that if everyone in the world lived as we do, it would take three planets to support us. Clearly, our way of life is not sustainable.

In selecting the sites, I have tried to select those that combine good quality information and are well-presented and easy-to-navigate. I have been particularly impressed by those that use multimedia to provide audio and video material, especially in the 'Global' section. The arguments are made more powerful when they are brought to life in this way and it's great to see the technology on our desktops put to such good use. If we have missed out any of your favourite sites, please contact us at info@southbankpublishing.com for inclusion in our next edition.

One word of warning: some of the sites encourage you to give information about yourself, join a forum or sign up for newsletters; others sell goods and services that you pay for online. It is important to keep yourself, your computer and your bank account safe. For some good advice go to **www.keepyourselfsafeonline.com**.

Acknowledgements

Thanks are due to Atherton, Katherine and Ali, who haven't complained when dinner is late and have endured hours of 'did you know' conversations while I've been writing this book.

Global

The environment

This section covers the sites that take a generalist approach to environmental issues, including sustainability, pollution, campaigning groups and government sites.

Government sites

The principle resource here is **www.environment-agency.gov.uk**, which has extensive sections on all the main environmental sectors. There is news about current events including business, science, research, agriculture and the environment. In addition, there are sections on flooding, conservation and water resources amongst other things, complete with subsections on the various topic components.

For a site aimed improving public awareness, the government have **www.direct.gov.uk/en/Environmentandgreenerliving/index.htm**, which has a straightforward approach to green and environmental issues and advice to encourage a more sustainable lifestyle. This is an excellent resource and a good starting point for a wide range of issues.

Other government sites:

www.britishecologicalsociety.org The British Ecological Society has several sections on their website that are of interest to the general public, including an introduction to ecology and ecological issues, following ecological stories that have come to the attention of the media and a section about ecological careers.

www.defra.gov.uk/environment A different viewpoint, this time from the Department for Environment and Rural Affairs. Here, the approach is more technical, aimed at those in agriculture and business; however, there is still a great deal on the site that is of interest to all concerned about sustainable development, country-side and wildlife, food, horticulture and the oceans.

www.jncc.gov.uk The Joint Nature Conservation Committee is a statutory advisor to government on national and international nature conservation. Have a look at the advice that they give; the information does not make for light reading, but this is as it should be.

www.nerc.ac.uk The Natural Environmental Research Council is responsible for funding and managing research, training and knowledge exchange in the environmental sciences. You can find out about the sorts of projects they fund and the themes that they are perusing. Under 'our research' the 'science highlights' are particularly interesting as they summarise the most exciting find-ings in previous years.

The daily news

Make **www.habitat.org.uk** your homepage for a daily British wildlife and environment e-zine. It picks up the news stories from all the various organisations and posts them on the one page.

Environmental organisations
www.cat.org.uk The Centre for Alternative Technology offers innovative, practical, sustainable solutions to many of the issues of everyday life, including reducing our energy consumption, water conservation and waste reduction. There is a wealth of ideas here, much of it free, but you do have to pay for the more detailed fact-sheets and booklets. They run courses on a wide range of topics and you can find out about their Graduate School of the Environment. It is not the easiest site to navigate, but persist and you'll probably find what you are looking for.

www.foe.co.uk The Friends of the Earth site has information about their campaigns on biodiversity, climate change, corporations, real food, trade, transport and waste. There is a huge amount of back data on the site, which can be accessed via their search engine; also check out details on how you can join in with their action.

www.forumforthefuture.org.uk This charity is committed to promoting sustainable development by working with businesses and organisations to effect change. Their current projects include one exploring what low carbon living will be like in 2022 and a sustainable cities index. An interesting site.

www.greenparty.org.uk The Green Party is a small ecological voice in the political wilderness, but they do have two representatives on the European Parliament and seven on the Scottish Parliament, plus many at a local level. On their website you can read about their policies and get involved.

www.greenpeace.org As the homepage says, 'Greenpeace exists because this fragile Earth deserves a voice. It needs solutions. It needs change. It needs actions.' There is a wealth of opportunity to take part in their actions as well as plenty of practical advice if you want to do it alone; if you are an armchair activist, watch the videos. Older campaigns and background research are also available through the search facility.

www.nature.org A US charity with over one million members, they aim to protect the world's priority conservation areas by working in partnerships with governments and communities to ensure biodiversity. There are some good articles on the site.

www.projectearth.com A very American site that is concerned about the adverse effect that man is having upon the Earth. Through a series of articles and news items, they strive to make the world a better place.

www.wen.org.uk The Women's Environmental Network aims to educate and empower women to make positive environmental change, and they campaign on environmental matters from a woman's perspective. In particular, they are interested in food, health and waste issues.

www.wri.org The US-based World Resources Institute is an environmental think tank that explores ways in which to protect the Earth and improve people's lives. There is some excellent material on the site, some of which comes in the form of information, some in a journalistic story format. Excellent.

Ecotalk

www.ecotalk.org.uk offers recordings of speeches on ecological topics, which you can download in MP3 format.

Resources and links

www.ace.mmu.ac.uk The Atmosphere, Climate and Environmental Information Programme was supported by DEFRA until 2005, since when it has not been updated. However, it remains a good resource even if some of the specifics are out of date.

www.allthingseco.co.uk A well-categorised eco directory listing 'thousands' of sites under the usual categories, with a section on the environment including climate change; carbon offsetting and woodland; conservation in the UK and worldwide; supporting charities; and world links. For an alternative try **www.ethicaldirectory.co.uk**, which has nearly 1,000 links in 169 categories.

www.ceh.ac.uk The Centre for Ecology and Hydrology researches and monitors terrestrial and freshwater environments. This is a huge resource for detailed scientific information and data, much of which is accessed by links to other sites. They have four programmes: biodiversity, water, biogeochemistry and environmental informatics; and two cross-cutting themes: climate change and sustainable economics.

www.ecoseek.net This is an American eco search engine, so some of the sites may not be applicable; however, it provides access to some quality material too.

www.envirolink.org The EnvironLink Network is a non-profit organisation that maintains a network of thousands of well-categorised environmental links on key environmental topics. It is also a grassroots online community that aims to unite organisations around the world.

Follow the eco-worrier

Check out Anna Shepard's column from *The Times* at **http://timesonline.typepad.com/eco_worrier**.

Pollution

www.airquality.co.uk This is an important site for anyone whose health is affected by poor air quality. The site provides current pollution levels and forecasts. In addition, there is information on how air quality is monitored, research reports and news. You can subscribe to the bulletins for daily forecasts and alerts.

www.ewg.org An excellent and detailed site from the Environmental Working Group dedicated to the fight against pollution. They have some research on their site that has extremely worrying findings, under subjects such as health and toxins, farming and natural resources. The section for parents is particularly informative and important.

Sustainable development and the community

www.green-space.org.uk A charity working to improve parks and green spaces for the wellbeing of all members of the community. They wish to ensure that in the future everyone has access to some green space and they will help to provide a network for the exchange of expertise in planning, design and park management. You can fill out an assessment of your local facilities at the site.

www.optimumpopulation.org A site that looks at the world and UK populations in terms of sustainability. It is run by a charity and boasts of having no political affiliations.

www.sustainable-development.gov.uk Recognition from the government that the model of development adopted over the past 20 years is unsustainable and that we are living beyond our means. The guiding principles of sustainable development are here, as are the UK priorities. There are links to other government sites, one of the more interesting of which is **www.communities.gov.uk/communities/sustainablecommunities**, which brings these policies and vision statements down to a local level.

www.sustainwales.com A directory of shops, businesses and organisations that have adopted a sustainable ethos. There is a good analysis of what sustainable living means for ordinary folk and stories that have been covered in the news.

www.sustdev.org Home of Sustainable Development International, a US organisation that provides reportage on key international issues and lobbies for sustainability at the UN and other main players in policy development. The most interesting section is 'issues', where you can find reports from all over the world.

An outstanding environmentalist

Read the essays, lectures and other writings of pioneering environmentalist James Lovelock, who saw the dangers of our lifestyle long before it was fashionable, at **www.jameslovelock.org**. In particular, look at his article from the *Guardian* dated 1 March 2008 in which he says that 'catastrophe is inevitable... and ethical living a scam'.

Scientific issues

http://genewatch.org A non-profit organisation that monitors the advance in genetic technology.

www.nanodot.org A US think tank on nanotechnology, advancing the cause of nanotechnology. They believe the technology has a role in supplying renewable energy, clean water and high-yield precision farming.

www.newscientist.com The website of *New Scientist* magazine, this is an excellent site to browse on a monthly basis to keep abreast of the latest scientific findings and observations. The special reports in the 'living world' section make particularly good reading.

Get it off your chest

If you've got an environmental sin to confess, go to **www.truegreenconfessions.com** and tell the world.

E-zines, community sites and blogs

There is a myriad of interactive sites for people of a green persuasion. There are a few listed here, but if you want more **www.bestgreenblogs.com** and **http://greenoptions.com** have plenty to offer. Most of them are American, so they might not all appeal, but there are some interesting thoughts and tips here from the other side of the pond – and you can add your own.

http://ethicaljobs.blogspot.com Interviews with a wide range of people working in the ethical sector.

http://greengirlsglobal.com An interesting collection of contributions and observations mainly from British women but some from other parts of the world.

http://lighterfootstep.com An American e-zine dedicated to sustainable living at home and in the workplace.

http://sustainablog.org An American blog on sustainable issues and environmental politics.

www.ecorazzi.com I guess someone had to start an eco celebrity site. Find out what the stars are doing to green their credentials.

www.green-trust.org A well-maintained site, run by a guy from New York, where people are encouraged to discuss sustainable living topics.

www.grist.org An e-zine devoted to nature and the environment in the broadest sense. It's well written and humorous in places, although it does have a very US bias and tone. One to browse.

www.juliahailes.com A good blog and rant site.

www.monbiot.com George Monbiot's site contains a number of articles written by the intrepid environmentalist and social commentator in his inimitable style. About four new articles appear each month, so it's well worth return visits.

www.thegreenguide.com Part of the *National Geographic* site with good articles, links to the environment section of their main site and a blog.

www.turnuptheheat.org The site related to the book by that name with an excellent exposé of greenwashing.

www.treehugger.com A popular site with news and features in an impressive range of categories, from celebrities to science and technology, business to politics. There's the chance to join in the forums, or go to **www.hugg.com** for user-submitted green news where there's a good collection of items to browse. It is American, so some of the material is not applicable.

www.off-grid.net A British community site featuring contributions on a wide range of topics with a forum to join and a small shop selling mainly solar-operated kit. We particularly liked the solar-powered sun umbrella that can be used to light your garden parties at night.

Facts

- The Isle of Eigg, off the Scottish coast, is the first fully self-sufficient island in the world as it now generates all its own electricity needs.

- Twenty of today's new cars generate the same amount of air pollution as one mid-1960s car.

- Over 80 per cent of marine pollution originated on land.

- Extreme global temperatures have risen by up to four degrees Celcius in the last 50 years, while the UK's temperature increases have been estimated at between point five and two degrees Celcius during the same period.

- Only 8 per cent of the world's ancient forests are currently under close protection.

- Raw sewage accounts for over 80 per cent of the pollution in India's rivers.

- The North Sea requires protected marine reserve areas covering 30 per cent in order to help rebuild the populations of many fish species.

- The UK's greenhouse gas emissions dropped by 2 per cent in 2007 from the previous year in line with Kyoto targets.

- There has been a 30 per cent shrinkage in the snow and ice cover in the eastern Himalayas since the 1970s.

- In 2005 the British spent more money on ethical products (including food, free-range eggs, green energy and eco body products) than they did on beer and cigarettes.

- Pesticide use worldwide has quadrupled in 40 years.

- The UK population has grown by more than a fifth since 1950.

- The world's population is projected to increase from the current 6.7 billion to 9.2 billion by 2050.

Climate change

No one reading this book can be unaware of the challenges we face due to climate change. There is a brief but well-written overview at **www.bbc.co.uk/climate** with links to interviews with some of the key players in the field of climate change. **www.metoffice.gov.uk** also has an excellent section on climate change with some good graphics and the opportunity to explore the subject in depth. There is also information about the current research undertaken at their Hadley Centre.

For a readable but more scientific viewpoint, The Royal Society at **www.royalsociety.org** takes a considered approach to the topic. There is background information and discussion about climate change controversies. In addition, they provide information on national and global policies and related links. In the section 'in my view' five eminent members of The Royal Society express their opinions regarding climate change and its impacts, which is interesting, if somewhat disquieting, reading.

A barometer on the world

The British Antarctic Survey site at **www.antarctica.ac.uk** has information regarding the impact of the warming Earth on this fragile continent. It's worth browsing the site to read diaries from those who are working there and to look at some of the stunning images.

Other recommended sites:

http://lwf.ncdc.noaa.gov The US National Climatic Data Center is the principle resource for climate information and data in the States. Although much of the information is US-based (interesting for those keen to follow their hurricane and tornado patterns), there is information on world weather, global climate events and historical climate data too.

www.algore.com The success of Al Gore's book and film *An Inconvenient Truth* has consolidated his position as a champion for action on climate change. Read his pages and even sign the 'Life Earth' pledge.

www.audubon.org/globalWarming This established American charity works for the preservation and wellbeing of wildlife but has a good section on global warming and its impact on the natural world.

www.ceh.ac.uk/sci_programmes/climate_change.html The Centre for Ecology and Hydrology provides information on their research projects.

www.climateark.org A messy site but a portal for content on global warming and climate change. There's some great material here, if you can find it.

www.climatechallenge.gov.uk The government's excellent pages on climate change with information and ideas on how you can get involved.

www.eci.ox.ac.uk For an academic approach, Oxford University Centre for the Environment's site is excellent and has links to their research projects, outreach projects and news clippings.

www.foe.co.uk For Friends of the Earth's take on the issues and the opportunity to join their campaign.

www.ghgonline.org One man's quest to provide an up-to-date resource dedicated to greenhouse gas news and scientific publications.

www.ipcc.ch The Intergovernmental Panel on Climate Change was established by the World Meteorological Organization to provide decision-makers with an objective source of information about climate change.

www.istl.org A substantial database of resources on climate change; huge and unwieldy it might be, but all the arguments are here.

www.open2.net/climatechange The online portal from the Open University and the BBC laden with interesting information and links. There are free OU courses in which to enrol, should you wish to take it further.

www.realclimate.org An independent commentary site on climate science by working climate scientists aimed at the interested public, this has some high-quality information that is not found on more populist sites. They have no political or campaigning focus; it's just pure science as they see it.

www.sd-commission.org.uk Website of the Sustainable Development Commission, the government's independent watchdog that produces evidence-based public reports on contentious environmental, social and economic issues, for example on nuclear power. The site provides an opportunity to influence policy and become involved at a national or local level.

www.stopclimatechaos.org A large coalition of organisations within the UK that have united to 'create an irresistible public mandate for political action to stop human-induced climate change'.

www.ukcip.org.uk The UK Climate Impacts Programme (UKCIP) provides scenarios that show how our climate might change and co-ordinates research on dealing with our future climate.

www.zsl.org/science/climate-change Climate change from the perspective of the Zoological Society of London, with information on the predicted impact on habitats in the UK and across the globe.

WWF One Planet Future campaign

The World Wildlife Fund has a coherent campaign designed to inspire individuals, businesses and governments to each play their part in reducing man's environmental impact on the planet. Join in at **www.wwf.org.uk**.

The argument against climate change

Apparently, only 90 per cent of scientists believe in human-induced climate change. Here are some places where you might find opposing views. The debate is summarised as a downloadable PDF entitled 'A Guide to Facts and Fictions about Climate Change' available at **www.royalsociety.org/downloaddoc.asp? id=1630**, where twelve 'misleading arguments' against climate change are debunked in a well-referenced article.

http://www.earthscape.org/p1/sdv01/sdv01e.html A dossier entitled 'The Case Against Human-Induced Climate Change – and Scientists' Response'.

www.globalwarming.org The Cooler Heads Coalition focuses on 'dispelling the myths of global warming by exposing flawed economic, scientific, and risk analysis'. An anti-legislation site with a negative view of Kyoto. Look under 'resources' for their position put most succinctly.

www.junkscience.com/news/robinson.htm An anti-Kyoto position.

www.marshall.org A US think tank, which has promoted scepticism about climate change. Read what they have to say; in particular, the PDF entitled 'Climate Issues and Questions' may be of interest.

In the news

The Times carries an article 'An experiment that hints we are wrong on climate change' at **www.timesonline.co.uk/tol/ news/uk/article1363818.ece**

Carbon offsetting

Carbon offsetting is the act of mitigating greenhouse gas emissions. This provides a means for businesses and individuals to assess their contribution to the 500 million tons of carbon dioxide produced annually by the UK. The schemes work by calculating an individual's carbon output and then taking a cash donation from them, which is used to support tree planting or research and development of renewable energy, energy conservation or methane capture schemes. For instance, **www.climatecare.org** calculate that a return flight from London to New York produces 1.54 tons of carbon dioxide per person. To offset this, a donation of £11.55 can be made to support schemes in the Third World.

Some think that these schemes make a positive contribution to the climate change agenda by raising awareness and enabling conservation or research, while other groups, such as Friends of the Earth, believe they hamper real change and encourage a lazy attitude instead of engendering a real change of lifestyle. Download their argument at **www.foe.co.uk/resource/briefing_notes/carbon_ offsetting.pdf**.

Carbon offsetting calculators
There are loads of companies now offering carbon calculators and the opportunity to support their schemes. The interactive one at **http://actonco2.direct.gov.uk/index.html** is really easy to follow, but here are a few alternatives:

www.carbon-clear.com

www.carbonneutral.com

www.climatecare.org

www.co2balance.uk.com

www.puretrust.org.uk

The voice of the future

Take a look at Effingham School's inspiring site, written with all the enthusiasm of youth, at **www.youthagainstclimatechange.org**.

What you can do

As well as offsetting and making practical changes in your consumption of energy (see page 50), there are other practical schemes that you can join to play an active part in mitigating climate change.

http://risingtide.org.uk A network of groups and individuals dedicated to taking local action against climate change. Locate a group near you or get help and advice on how to set one up. They have some excellent online resources to download including a template speech on climate change and advice on handling the media.

www.climatefriends.org.uk Promoted by the Somerset branch of the Wildlife Trust, this site encourages you to become a 'climate friend' by taking five practical steps in your life.

www.climateprediction.net The largest experiment to try and produce an accurate forecast of the climate in the twenty-first century, using the spare capacity of personal computers. You allow them to run a climate predication model from your computer when it is not being used to optimum capacity and in return you get to watch the results on your computer.

www.foe.co.uk/campaigns/climate/big_ask/about.html As well as offering some practical suggestions, Friends of the Earth have set up 'The Big Ask' to lobby for new, more effective laws on emissions.

www.greenpeace.org.uk/climate/what-you-can-do Join the consummate campaigning group Greenpeace.

www.icount.org.uk The public wing of Stop Climate Chaos with the motto 'Together we are irresistible – together we count'. The site has loads of news and events. Check out their interactive map for organisations in your area.

www.naturescalendar.org.uk Phenology is the study of recurring natural phenomena such as the sighting of the first snowdrops or song thrush. By plotting the changes over the years, scientists can study the impact of climate change on wildlife. The up-to-date maps are particularly interesting as they enable you to see what is happening in real time. You can become a recorder at the site.

Arrange a meeting and get a speaker

www.climate-speakers.org.uk

Aimed at business

www.businessclimatechampions.org This site is sponsored by the Association of Town Centre Management and is designed to provide businesses with the knowledge and solutions they need to understand and react to climate change.

www.climatecare.org Aims to help businesses appreciate the benefits of emission reductions and price the cost of carbon into their budgets. They offer a range of services depending on the size of the company. The site has a number of case studies as examples, a list of companies that have used their services and a business carbon dioxide calculator.

www.carbonsense.org.uk Good advice on how businesses can move towards a low-carbon future and motivate their workforce.

www.carbontrust.co.uk Primarily supports the development of low carbon technologies and helps business and the public sector cut carbon emissions. They will carry out a free on-site survey of your company's carbon footprint and offer practical solutions.

www.panda.org Follow the link 'how we work' to a good section on their work with companies that are committed to sustainability.

Blog

Dr Glen Barry has an interesting blog at **www.climateark.org/blog** as part of the Climate Ark site, which is a portal devoted to climate change and global warming.

Facts

- Approximately 20 per cent of emissions each year are from deforestation and forest fires.

- Over 80 per cent of the weight of fuel is made up of carbon. Each carbon atom reacts with two oxygen atoms taken from the air as it burns. As oxygen atoms are more than twice as heavy as carbon atoms, the emissions generated by burning one kilogram of fuel weighs over three kilograms.

- Carbon dioxide levels in the Earth's atmosphere have increased by 30 per cent in the last 200 years.

- Global temperatures have risen by over 0.7 degrees Celcius since the 1700s; half a degree of this warming has occurred during the past 100 years.

- Sea levels are predicted to rise by 28 to 43 centimetres by the end of this century.

- Unless radical action is taken, global energy demands could rise by as much as 60 per cent in the next 20 years.

- Experts predict that global warming could shrink the global economy by 20 per cent.

- As a result of global warming, melting glaciers could cause water shortages for one in six of the world's population.

- In the UK, 98 per cent of the population are aware of the climate change issue, and 81 per cent are concerned about it.

- Some 90 million people are added to the planet each year.

Ecology and the natural world

Man's activities are diminishing natural habitats and biodiversity at an unprecedented rate. To assess the state of the planet the World Wildlife Fund issues a 'Living Planet' report, which makes worrying reading. You'll find it at **www.panda.org** – follow the link to publications. There is a massive amount of other interesting material on their site and some fabulous photographs to remind us why we should sign up and join their campaigns. They have an interesting project on threatened habitats that focuses on a 'priority species'. These are species chosen to represent the threat to an eco-region and, by improving the habitat for that species, others that are vulnerable to the same threats are helped to survive.

Ecology and conservation in the UK

There are a number of organisations working within the UK to protect our natural environment and biodiversity.

www.bbc.co.uk/earth/nature/uk The BBC have reorganised their resources and plants seem to have been subsumed by animals. However, this site is a joy to browse. Search the A–Z index for the range of activities on the site and the map locator to find wildlife of interest in your area or one you plan to visit. There are guided walks, wildlife spectaculars, events, videos and blogs. If you return to the 'Science and Nature' section of the site, you can also find their pages on UK wildlife, which contain many more sections including the Springwatch and Autumnwatch links. You can even download a Mini Oddi onto your desktop who will give you UK wildlife updates. There are more serious offerings on habitats and some excellent material on natural history worldwide.

www.bna-naturalists.org The British Naturalists' Association has a gentle site that covers its work and provides some identification guides and information on phenology. Join Professor David Bellamy and become a member of the society, or even a take up the opportunities to volunteer.

www.britishecologicalsociety.org An interesting resource, particularly helpful to serious students and teachers of ecology. The society provides teaching resources, academic journals, sponsorships and grants, and facilitates research.

www.cpre.org.uk The Campaign to Protect Rural England works for a sustainable future for the English countryside. You can find out about their current campaigns on the site and join the organisation. Their well-categorised library is a useful resource for anyone wishing to find out more about matters pertinent to the countryside and sustainable development. Some of the publications are free; some can also be downloaded; others you need to purchase. See also **www.ruralscotland.org** for Scotland, **www.cprw.org.uk** for Wales, and **www.countrysideni.org** for Northern Ireland.

www.habitas.org.uk The Ulster Museum has a huge resource on the flora and fauna of Northern Ireland.

www.naturalengland.org.uk Natural England (formally English Nature) works towards creating a healthy natural environment that is sustainably managed and is enjoyed and understood by the public. In their 'conservation' section there is information about the biodiversity actions plans and how they intend to enforce them. There is also a good introduction to local geology on a county-by-county basis and the geodiversity action plans, which aim to conserve the very ground we walk on. For Scotland, **www.snh.org.uk** is an excellent site, and **www.wildlifewales.co.uk** offers a similar resource for Wales.

www.ptes.org The People's Trust for Endangered Species is mainly concerned about the preservation of British wildlife, although it does sponsor some overseas work. Find out how you can get involved in their events.

www.uksafari.com This website states that there's well in excess of 1,000 pages of info and around 3,000 photos on the site. As well as information on animals and plants, there is a good section on photography. It makes for an interesting browse and you can submit your wildlife photographs, send e-cards and sign up for their free newspaper.

www.wildlifetrusts.org The umbrella organisation that covers the 47 regional local Wildlife Trusts, which campaign for better protection for indigenous wildlife and habitats. The site links with the local organisations, and you can find out about visiting their reserves and joining in with local events and activities.

www.wwt.org.uk The Wildfowl and Wetlands Trust is a conservation charity and their site has good information on the habitats that they are seeking to preserve. In the section 'learn' there are fact files on wetlands and associated wildlife, sustainability, ecology and conservation issues.

www.zsl.org The Zoological Society of London is more than just a zoo. There are details here of their scientific activities, their field conservation projects and a section on the work of the modern zoo.

Be part of the next earthday

Go to **ww2.earthday.net**.

Ecology and conservation worldwide

www.awf.org The African Wildlife Foundation works in the African heartlands on conservation and land preservation issues. The site has interesting species information and details of their programme.

www.bbc.co.uk/nature/animals *Planet Earth* is here for a start, with downloadable clips and an explorer that enables you to access interactive videos. There's a wildlife blog, as well as a plethora of articles and features on animals, plants, birds and conservation. Use the search engine if you have a particular area of interest or you'll be sidetracked on this fascinating site.

www.conservation.org Conservation International have a well-presented site about the conservation work they do worldwide. They explain the issues and how they go about their work. There are written, spoken and video reports from their fieldworkers and some stunning photography.

www.footprintnetwork.org A Canadian organisation that has developed a strategy called 'ecological footprint' that measures the ecological resource use and capacity of each nation. Armed with this knowledge, and working with governments, cities and businesses, they can then help nations reduce their footprint year on year.

www.fws.gov The Fish and Wildlife Service; Audubon (**www.audubon.org**), a well-established natural history charity; and the National Wildlife Federation (**www.nwf.org**) are US-based organisations concerned principally with their own wildlife.

www.panda.org Although this site has been mentioned previously in reference to biodiversity, it is worth referring to their 'where we work' section for extensive coverage of issues worldwide. Their search engine is useful if there is a particular animal or region that you wish to find.

www.wcs.org The Wildlife Conservation Society's mission is to save wildlife and wild lands. As well as running zoos, the society does conservation work throughout the world and has some fascinating pages on the countries in which it works and the animals that it helps. **www.wildnet.org** is another American charity with a similar but less extensive mission.

www.world.org Useful for its 'top 1,000 websites' resource.

Eco philosophy

For an intellectual discussion of the philosophical issues surrounding ecology visit **www.thegreenfuse.org**.

Biodiversity

The variety of life on Earth from micro-organisms to whales is under threat and species loss is continuing at alarming speed. If you need convincing go to **www.well.com/~davidu/extinction.html** for a huge list of scientific and popular press articles on the subject.

Many of the UK and international sites do contain a huge amount of material about biodiversity, but the following are more specialist sites. For a brief introduction to biodiversity go to The Natural History Museum site at **www.nhm.ac.uk/nature-online** and follow the links. The section on environmental change is equally useful.

http://extinct.petermaas.nl This site is dedicated to the animals and plants for which it is too late. There are lists of extinctions in the various parts of the world, articles on extinction, the causes of extinction and possible revival strategies.

http://tolweb.org/tree The Tree of Life web project is a collaborative project involving biologists from around the world. The site boasts more than 9,000 web pages, featuring information about the diversity of life on Earth. It isn't the easiest site to navigate, but the information you are seeking is probably here; it's best to use the search engine.

www.biodiversityhotspots.org Conservation International provides a fabulous site that focuses on 34 hotspots that are under threat. If you click on the interactive map it takes you to a detailed micro-site about the area at risk. You can sign up for their newsletter too.

www.catalogueoflife.org The goal of this site is to create a 2008 checklist of all the known species (plants, animals, fungi and microbes). You can check out their progress on the site.

www.mnh.si.edu/explore/diversity.htm A detailed offering from the Smithsonian Museum of Natural History. Some of the links take you to other mini sites; others give a huge amount of information on the selected topics including factsheets, audio samples, images, lifecycle information and a look at the case in the museum, where appropriate.

www.nbn.org.uk The National Biodiversity Network's aim is to collect together biodiversity information and make species data accessible through their new website.

The rainforest

Conserving the rainforest is absolutely central to the future of the world as we know it. Not only are the forests' role in the rain cycle and the carbon cycle vital to our existence, but the ten million species of plants, animals and insects that live there deserve our protection and understanding. Many of the rainforest plants may indeed have medicinal properties that we will never discover if we allow them to be destroyed. However, in the last 50 years we've obliterated around half of the rainforests and are continuing to burn the rest at an alarming rate. Understanding rainforest conservation and supporting the cause is imperative.

www.dendronautics.org This site is devoted to the study of the rainforest canopy from the air using airships and aerial platforms. There are some videos from previous missions, plenty of pictures and links.

www.rainforest-alliance.org A good starting point for information and links to related sites, with lots of news and background on major rainforest projects.

Get the mag

Check out **www.theecologist.org** for the online version of the *Ecologist* magazine – the dilemmas section is particularly thought-provoking.

---

www.rainforestconcern.org Your chance to sponsor an acre of rainforest. Follow the fate of **www.twomenplantaforest.co.uk**, which is an associated project.

www.rainforestportal.org A good starting point to begin any research into the rainforest with a well-categorised lists of links. See also **http://forests.org** – a messy site to read and the links are the same as in rainforestportal, but the Forest Protection blog is worth a browse.

www.worldlandtrust.org The trust has helped to save over 142,000 hectares (350,000 acres) of rainforest and wildlife habitats world-wide. The webcam is wonderful and the virtual tours and videos make full use of the technology.

Facts

- The World Wildlife Fund's 'terrestrial species index' showed a 31 per cent decline from 1970 to 2003.

- More than 90 per cent of the world's tiger population disappeared in the last century.

- The Wildlife Trust's combined membership is in excess of 726,000 members, making it the largest voluntary organisation in the UK.

- Giraffes have declined in numbers by an estimated 30 per cent in the last ten years.

- During the 1970s and '80s nearly half of Africa's elephants were killed for ivory.

- Over 100 of the world's 260 species of turtles are in decline.

- Indonesia is home to 17 per cent of the world's bird species, 12 per cent of the mammals, 16 per cent of the reptiles and amphibians and 33 per cent of all the world's insects. Unfortunately, it is also home to many tree species desirable to loggers.

- The tallest trees in the rainforest can grow to 70 metres.

- In excess of 20 per cent (some estimates are nearly 30 per cent) of the world's carbon dioxide emissions come from slashing and burning the forests.

- The Amazon forest stores and recycles half of the world's fresh water.

Animals

This section is devoted to wildlife, although many of the sites mentioned in the 'Environment' and 'Ecology and the natural world' sections (pages 9 and 25) have relevance here. Many of these sites make excellent use of technology, featuring some amazing audio clips, video footage, webcams and, of course, some magnificent photography.

General animal sites

http://animaldiversity.ummz.umich.edu A fabulous site from the University of Michigan Museum of Zoology with a vast amount of hidden information. To see what they have to offer go to 'about us' and 'overview' to find out about their searchable encyclopaedia and their virtual museum, which strangely are not featured on their interactive index. Under 'special topics' is an incredible collection of skulls, many of them annotated with background information and noises, where appropriate.

http://ibc.hbw.com/ibc An audiovisual library of the world's birds with fantastic footage of common and extraordinary birds. They claim to cover 50 per cent of the global species. Use the search facility to find the birds you are interested in, or browse the new additions or highlights. If you have footage worthy of posting on the site, they are happy to accept contributions.

www.africam.com/wildlife/index.php Check out the webcams located at sites selected to maximise the possibility of catching a glimpse of some of the continent's greatest wildlife attractions. If time doesn't allow you to sit and watch at a watering hole, view the highlights. For species information, go to **www.africanfauna.com**, which is slightly on the dull side but covers a good selection of creatures.

www.animalsasia.org A Hong Kong-based animal welfare charity that cares for wild, domestic and endangered species in Asia. Has some harrowing information on Chinese bear farming and their rescue mission.

www.antarcticconnection.com This internet 'e-tailer' has some good information on the wildlife and science of the Antarctic. Great for penguins and albatrosses, and news.

www.australian-animals.net A great place to discover the facts about Australia's unique wild animals with some good accompanying photographs; while **www.australianfauna.com** has similar information.

www.davidshepherd.org David Shepherd has a reputation for his art and his passion for animals. This has been translated into action by the setting up of this wildlife foundation. The site has details on the foundation's work in Africa and Asia.

www.nationalgeographic.com/animals This is not exclusively an environmental site; however, many of their features are of interest and their photos are magnificent. The A–Z of animals is a great resource.

www.uksafari.com A good place for an introduction to the wildlife and countryside of Britain. There are over 1,000 pages of information, 3,000 pictures and a collection of video clips.

Endangered species

(See also the section 'Biodiversity' on page 29).

http://bagheera.com A beautiful site aimed at preserving the animals that are vanishing in the wild. The information on each animal and the causes of its decline is good and their 'spotlight' topics put the crisis into context, exploring factors such as climate change, Asian medicines and human population growth.

http://wildlifedirect.org A charity devoted to endangered species in Africa. There is an extensive list of field blogs, videos with blogs and videos.

www.arkive.org ARKive describes itself as the 'Noah's Ark for the internet era'. It consists of a digital library of films, photographs and audio recordings of the world's species, and it is a fantastic resource. Type in the animal that you are investigating and a list of movies and images appears. They have a special chapter on endangered species and another on British wildlife, both common and at risk. Its parent organisation is **www.wildscreen.org.uk**, which has a mission to promote the public appreciation of biodiversity and conservation through wildlife imagery.

www.endangeredspecie.com An American site with good photography and background information on the causes of species decline and profiles of animals at risk.

www.kidsplanet.org/factsheets/map.html Aimed at children, but provides basic factsheets on endangered animals of the world.

www.ptes.org The People's Trust for Endangered Species works to halt species loss worldwide but with a UK focus. They run a programme of events to enable people to both observe their work and get involved. You can sign up on the site. If you want to become a mammal species recorder you could also look into the Mammal Society at **www.abdn.ac.uk/mammal**.

www.rarespecies.org An organisation that devises conservation strategies; it's very interesting to find out how it's done.

www.redlist.org The World Conservation Union's site provides a searchable database of threatened species and masses of technical material on the process of the classification of animals for the 'red list' of endangered animals. It has a very extensive collection of links.

Information on species conservation

The Smithsonian Zoological Park has a database of animals at **http://nationalzoo.si.edu/Animals/AnimalIndex**. Check out the alphabetical list of animals for information on a huge selection of animals. The conservation status of each is given, along with facts and links.

Here are some of the animals at risk (marine life is covered in the 'Oceans' section on page 43).

Amphibians and reptiles

www.crocodilian.com

www.herpconbio.org

Apes

www.chimps-inc.org; www.janegoodall.org

www.gorilla.org

www.unep.org/grasp

Bats

www.bats.org.uk

Bears

www.bbc.co.uk/nature/animals/conservation/bears

www.nativehabitats.org/bears.htm

Big cats

www.bornfree.org.uk

www.cheetahspot.com

www.savethetigerfund.org

www.st-andrews.ac.uk/~pga/feline/bigcats.html

Birds

www.barnowltrust.org.uk

www.bto.org

www.rspb.org.uk

www.ornithology.com

Butterflies and moths

http://ukmoths.org.uk

www.butterfly-conservation.org

www.mothcount.brc.ac.uk

Dormice

www.glirarium.org/dormouse

Elephants

http://elephant.elehost.com

www.changthai.com

www.elephantconservation.org

www.elephanttrust.org

www.sheldrickwildlifetrust.org (also rhinos)

Giraffes

www.isidore-of-seville.com/giraffe

Hedgehogs

www.britishhedgehogs.org.uk

Insects

www.bugbios.com

www.buglife.org.uk

Pandas

http://nationalzoo.si.edu/Animals/GiantPandas

Polar bears

www.polarbearsinternational.org

Squirrels

www.highlandredsquirrel.co.uk

www.redsquirrels.info

Turtles and tortoises

www.chelonia.org

www.turtleconservation.org

Wolves

www.justgiving.com/wildcru-ewolf

www.ukwolf.org

www.wolftrust.org.uk

Wild animal protection organisations

www.animal.org.uk Join a campaign to stop the exploitation of animals.

www.ifaw.org Home of the excellent International Fund for Animal Welfare.

www.traffic.org A campaigning site working against the illegal and sometimes appalling trade in animals throughout the world.

www.ufaw.org.uk Improving animal welfare using scientific knowledge.

Facts

- **At least 200,000 turtles (worth around $1 million) are traded every year in Vietnam.**

- **There have been five major mass extinctions in the Earth's history.**

- **Rainforests covered around 14 per cent of the Earth's land surface until a few thousand years ago; now it is just over 2 per cent.**

- **A four-square-mile (1,000 hectare) area of rainforest contains up to 1,500 species of flowering plants, 750 species of trees, 125** species of mammals, 400 species of birds, 150 species of butter-flies, 100 species of reptiles and 60 species of amphibians.

- Background extinction levels are estimated to be from one to ten species per year for the past 600 million years due to the natural processes of evolution.

- There are more than 1,000 animals considered endangered worldwide.

- There are more than 3,500 protected areas in existence world-wide; together, they cover around 3 per cent of the total land area of the planet.

- In the UK the mammals most under threat are water voles, red squirrels, wildcats, pine martens, greater horseshoe bats, Barbastelle bats, Bechstein's bats, bottle-nose dolphins, harbour porpoises and northern right whales.

Plants

The preservation of plants is vital for the planet's wellbeing. Plants generate the oxygen we breathe, filter out the warming gas, carbon dioxide, and form the basis of the food chain on which all animals depend. With one in eight of the world's plants assessed to be at risk, there is much work for the conservationists to do.

The Eden Project

Man's interdependence on plants is showcased at the Eden Project, **www.edenproject.com**, which explores this relationship and the issues surrounding it. This site is a good starting point for an overview of the plant world and man's relationship with it; the information is simply stated and burning issues such as climate change, sustainability, biodiversity, genetic modification, and food and agriculture are all explored.

At the Eden Project they grow in excess of a million plants, repre-senting over 5,000 species. Many of these are grown in massive

Biomes (in essence, giant greenhouses), which enables them to grow plants from many of the world's climatic zones. In one sense, this is an elaborate plant theme park, but underpinning the wow factor is their mission to educate the public and their academic rigor. They are a catalyst for scientific work not just on site, but in universities and in practical conservation projects around the world. Details of the work that they undertake can be found under 'projects' in the 'foundation' section of the website and can be further investigated through their links.

Under 'horticulture' the contents of the various Biomes are explored, not only from a genus point of view, but with a focus on the practical use of plants. For instance, we learn that citrus plants have antibacterial properties, can be used as a CFC substitute and are used in the perfume industry. We are also alerted to the fact that watering citrus crops can have severe ecological consequences. More familiar plants are found in the outside Biome, along with other plants that can exist naturally in the Cornish climate. Here industries such as brewing, dying and growing plants for fuel are investigated and there are sections devoted to developing garden plants and the flowerless garden, which covers the ancient species that existed prior to the evolution of flowering plants.

The scope of the project is vast and the site reveals just a tip of the iceberg; however, it successfully removes plants from the realm of the dull and irrelevant and whets the appetite to visit and learn more.

General sites

The following sites are dedicated to plant life alone. For information on the genetic modification debate, see page 14. Of course, many of the sites recommended under the sections on the environment (page 9), the natural world and ecology (page 25), and gardening (page 88) also cover plant life.

www.bgci.org Botanic Gardens Conservation International leads global efforts to protect plants and try to reverse the impending extinction crisis. The site details their work and has some of their research reports to download. There is a lot more information on the site than first appears; use the search engine to help you find your way around.

www.british-trees.com This site has information on native trees with good links. Some of the trees are pictured along with shots of leaves, flowers and seeds; however, it is a shame that not all the trees are fully illustrated.

www.britmycolsoc.org.uk This describes itself as a 'learned society' and there is not much here for the general reader, but under 'resources' there are links and details on publications, some of them downloadable, and in 'education' you can find out where to go for courses and links to other mycology sites including **www.fungionline.org.uk** – their sponsored site, which has lots of information about the biology of fungi.

www.globaltrees.org Learn about the projects that the Global Trees Campaign is undertaking. There is a profile of trees under threat with information about their habitat, its uses and why it is threatened.

www.internationaltreefoundation.org.uk This foundation promotes an appreciation of trees by supporting a range of projects that plant, care for and protect trees. You can find out about tree-planting grants and how to apply for a tree preservation order. They also promote a number of international projects. Find out if there is a local branch for you to join or that might be able to help a community project near you. Should you donate to them, there is possibility of having an area designated by a name of your choice.

www.kew.org You could start a visit to this site by taking their tour of the gardens, which leads you through the various sections of the garden and provides details about the plants that you encounter. Alternatively, look under 'collections' then 'garden overviews' to arrive at the 'explore Kew' pages, where there is a list of the plant groups that they grow with background information on the plant, its botanical history and links to other relevant sections on the site.

There is a huge amount of information in this section that is of interest to the botanist and the casual browser and, if they don't grow specimens of the plants themselves, they refer you to Kew's Electronic Plant Information Centre for references. **www.kew.org/conservation** is Kew Gardens' section on conservation and sustainable use. It includes a phenology database, information about their research and links to overseas projects. There is a link to a mini site on their Millennium Seed Bank Project, which aims to bank seed from 10 per cent of the world's plants in the next decade. They explain the science and technology behind the project and you can search the database.

www.nccpg.com The National Council for the Conservation of Plants and Gardens has a searchable database to enable you to find a species in the National Collections. There is a section on the naming of plants, which is aimed at the holders of the national collections, but might be of interest to the committed amateur. Their basic botany section is a good resource too.

www.plantaeuropa.org The European Plant Conservation Strategy is on this site. It is very dry and not aimed at the general reader.

www.plantlife.org.uk Plantlife is the only charity working solely to protect Britain's wild flowers, plants, fungi and lichens, and the habitats in which they are found. A section on the 'Plant Diversity Challenge' sets out the objectives of this initiative, which has the conservation of plant species at its heart. There are also reports on species under their care and information on how to get involved.

www.uksafari.com This site has good descriptive material on ferns, fungi, galls, lichens, moss, trees and wildflowers. Basic information on each plant is provided, along with accompanying photographs.

www.woodland-trust.org.uk A charitable trust dedicated to the preservation of Britain's native woodland. They own or have stewardship over 1,100 woods in the country and are creating new areas of native woodland.

Virtual botany

Visit the top botanical gardens in the world. Get the preview and links to each garden's site at **www.travelandleisure.com/ articles/great-botanical-gardens-of-the-world**.

Facts

- Ten per cent of the world's tree species are under threat.

- Of the 345 British wild plant species assessed, almost 20 per cent are currently threatened with extinction.

- Fifty years ago Chinese farmers were growing 10,000 different varieties of wheat; by 1970 this was down to 1,000.

- Fewer than 1 per cent of plant species have been screened for bio-active compounds.

- Only about 200,000 of the estimated 1–1.5 million species of fungi have been described.

- Of the 7,000 plant species found in South Africa's southern cape, more than 1,400 are considered to be critically rare, endangered or vulnerable.

- In the last 100 years, 46 broadleaved woodland species have become extinct in the UK.

- Only 12 per cent of the UK is woodland; the European average is 44 per cent.

Oceans

The oceans are under threat from a variety of pressures: principally over-fishing, pollution from sewage, pollution from shipping, radioactive waste and aggregate exploitation. Anyone who is in doubt should go to the fabulous five-part multimedia presentation from the *LA Times* at **www.latimes.com/news/local/oceans/la-oceans-series,0,7842752.special**, which has articles, videos, photos and graphics.

The best all-round site for information on the oceans as habitats and the creatures that depend on them is **www.mcsuk.org**, the Marine Conservation Society site. Here you will find details of their conservation work along with information on the major conservation threats. Although not highly illustrated, the quality of the information is good.

Here are some other useful sites:

www.bbc.co.uk/nature/blueplanet A highly designed approach from the BBC, this site has a good range of feature articles on ocean life. The best bit is the *Blue Plant* television series section: you can see previews of the programme, (unfortunately not in its entirety), read a cogent synopsis of the programme and get facts about the creatures that they encountered, including their conservation status. There are also 'factfiles' on oceanography and a whole lot of cartoon games.

www.flmnh.ufl.edu/fish The University of Florida's Department of Ichthyology has a fascinating site where, amongst the huge amount of information available, you can find an overview of fish species including pictures and links. The section on sharks and the kids sections are particularly good.

www.marlin.ac.uk The Marine Life Information Network for Britain and Ireland has good species information on native flora and fauna. You can see the work that they have done on the 'sensitivity scales' which ranks the various habitats and species according to their vulnerability. You are also encouraged to become a volunteer recorder.

www.noaa.gov The US National Oceanic and Atmospheric Administration is a resource for material on oceanic matters. It is not easy to negotiate, but there is good information to be found.

www.oceanconserve.org Ocean Conserve is a portal and search engine that is useful for finding specific information.

Shark news

Read the *Guardian*'s 'Shark species face extinction' article at **www.guardian.co.uk/environment/2008/feb/18/conservation.a aas**.

Organisations

http://see-the-sea.org A marine awareness organisation that aims to promote the reversal of human-caused environmental damage and help to revive and preserve the ocean ecosystem. There is some good material on the site threaded with links.

www.davidsuzuki.org/Oceans A Canadian conservation charity which has some good pages on the subject.

www.greenpeace.org.uk/oceans For many the archetypal image of Greenpeace is that of the *Rainbow Warrior* ships chasing after Japanese whalers. See how their campaigns are progressing with their new boats.

www.sas.org.uk Surfers Against Sewage – anyone who surfs can understand why this site exists. Their campaign extends to all sorts of marine pollution, including oil from shipping, toxic chemicals in the sea and marine litter. They are also concerned about climate change and the changes it may bring, not only to the oceans, but to their watersport. There are links to related articles too.

www.seashepherd.org A conservation group based in Oregon that sends a boat out to fight the cause of marine mammals, particularly whales. Follow their missions here.

Community sites and ezines

www.scripps.ucsd.edu Scripps Institution of Oceanography's website, where you can sign up for their e-zine 'explorations', which has some good articles.

www.shiftingbaselines.org A media project linking ocean conservation and Hollywood, aimed at drawing attention to the perilous state of the oceans. There are news stories, a photo competition and humour; they even have their own symphony orchestra. An odd site, but one with a mission. See also their blog at **http://scienceblogs.com/shiftingbaselines**.

Marine life at risk

Coral reefs

> **http://oceanworld.tamu.edu/students/coral/index.html**
>
> **www.coralcay.org/science**
>
> **www.iyor.org**
>
> **www.reefrelief.org**

Sharks

> **http://baskingsharks.wildlifetrusts.org**
>
> **www.sharkandcoralconservation.com**
>
> **www.sharks.org**
>
> **www.sharktrust.org**

Seahorses

> **www.theseahorsetrust.co.uk**

Turtles

> **www.seaturtles.org**
>
> **www.turtleconservation.org**
>
> **www.turtles.org**

Whales and dolphins

> **www.idw.org**
>
> **www.oceanalliance.org**
>
> **www.seawatchfoundation.org.uk**

www.wdcs.org

www.wwf.org.au/ourwork/oceans/whales

Facts

- Marine plants produce half the Earth's oxygen.

- Only 4 per cent of the ocean is untouched by man's activities.

- Around 2.5 million tons of oil-derived pollution finds its way into the oceans each year.

- Ten per cent of the world's coral reefs have been destroyed.

- Since 1960 warm water plankton species have moved north by ten degrees latitude.

- Nine species of sharks are at the top of the list of marine animals that could be extinct in the next 30 years.

- The ocean covers 71 per cent of the planet.

- Nearly 50 per cent of all species on Earth live in the oceans.

- The temperature of the North Sea has risen by 0.6 degrees Celcius in the past 40 years. In response, North Sea fish have moved north.

- Beluga whales in the St Lawrence Estuary, Canada are so heavily contaminated with PCBs that their carcasses are classified as toxic waste.

Domestic

E-zines, directories and blogs

There are a number of sites which cover the entire spectrum of domestic and personal life and do not easily slot into any one category. These include e-zines and sites that have a general environmental living theme and directories – just in case this book fails to find one to answer your needs.

General sites

http://eartheasy.com An American e-zine with a good feel to it. You may not want to shop on the site but you can find easily accessible advice and articles on all things domestic. You could usefully pass quite a bit of time browsing this site.

www.ecotipoftheday.com Sign up and you'll get a tip of the day, obviously.

www.greenliving.co.uk A minimally designed collection of articles that are intended to provide positive examples of things people have done to green-up their lifestyles.

www.grownupgreen.org.uk A sensible and well-organised e-zine with news and features and a library of back articles on energy, living spaces, transport, waste and know-how. A good place to visit on a regular basis for news and ideas on what is happening in towns and cities across the country. There is a small shop and should you become a member you can submit your own articles and get a newsletter too.

www.sustainablestuff.co.uk For straightforward features and advice about a greener lifestyle written by professionals.

www.theenvironmentsite.org This interactive site has an eco blog, a discussion forum and a number of green living guides, eco tips and environmental sources to offer. If you shop online through them you'll raise funds for the site.

Directories

www.allthingseco.co.uk A directory site with 'thousands' of links to green and ethical companies organised in a large number of categories. There is also information on green issues and eco news. An excellent resource.

www.ecological-living.co.uk A good green directory and information site with articles and news features.

www.guidemegreen.com Another green and ethical listing site with a UK directory, jobs, courses, a forum and articles.

www.hitfix.co.uk/environment A directory of environmentally aware sites for products, services and information.

www.onegreenearth.com An eco-portal to 'unite people in their quest for a sustainable future'. This is a small directory of links to eco-friendly businesses and suppliers with a few articles and a shop.

Blogs

http://bean-sprouts.blogspot.com An inspiring account of a family's attempts at the green life. It has posts from their small home, garden, allotment, bees and chickens. There is an impressive list of categorised back blogs to peruse.

www.selfsufficientish.com The urban guide to almost self-sufficiency with a personal feel. There is a forum if you want to contribute and an encyclopaedia of articles.

Energy

Energy consumption and climate change are geo-political hot potatoes. Globally, the problems are huge and raise all kinds of complicated moral and economic difficulties; hence the tortuous deliberations at the Bali and Kyoto conferences. But scale the problem down and this is an area where individual households can make a significant difference.

The Energy Saving Trust's website at **www.energysavingtrust. org.uk** is a good starting point. It offers a comprehensive look at the issues in the domestic context and provides good, practical solutions. They have a product comparison service and an online home energy check, and they suggest home improvements. There is an excellent postcode search facility that enables you to track down grants and offers for energy-saving improvements. Also check out the Centre for Alternative Technology's site at **www.cat.org.uk**; go and visit or just take inspiration from a detail-rich website.

Green tariffs

It takes very little time to change energy suppliers and there are a number of green tariffs available. They differ in their approach, but usually agree to source a higher percentage of energy from renewable generation, per unit of electricity used, than normal suppliers. Some offer green funds, which support the construction of renewable energy facilities or fund environmental causes. Many also agree to carbon offsetting (see page 21). Be aware that some green tariffs draw on nuclear power, which you may not support.

To begin a tariff trawl try **www.greenenergy.uk.com**. Type in your postcode, then up pop the green suppliers in your area. They provide excellent information on pricing and the fuel mix used by each provider, and pass verdict on the company's green credentials. **http://green.energyhelpline.com/energy** offers a similar service.

The Severn Barrage

For information on harnessing wave energy on the River Severn, look at **http://en.wikipedia.org/wiki/Severn_Barrage**.

Alternative energy

Alternative energy sources offer a clean substitute for carbon-generating fossil fuels. Renewable energy implies that the source of the energy is constantly replenished and includes wind, water, solar and geothermal power. There are also the more controversial alternative fuels such as nuclear, biomass, incineration of waste and bio-fuels. None of these sources are without environmental impact; for instance, the destruction of natural habitats for hydro-electric production, bird kill in wind turbines and the problem of radioactive waste from nuclear plants. A simple summary can be found at **www.netpilot.ca/aes**, while **www.envocare.co.uk/ alternative_energy.htm** has more detail on an unattractively designed site.

Households can make a contribution to their own energy needs by installing solar panels or a small wind turbine. A few new builds use geothermal technologies, which are harder to integrate into existing homes, but it can be done. **www.earthpeace.co.uk** is good for inspiration and information on the options and how they work.

Here are some additional links:

http://c-zero.co.uk Supplies a wide range of technologies and information, as do **www.wirefreedirect.com** and **www. alternativeenergystore.co.uk**.

www.cse.org.uk A charitable company with a mission to educate and enable individuals and communities to seek alternative energy solutions and promote sustainable policies and practices.

www.ecocentre.org.uk/selling-electricity-back-to-the-grid.html If you generate more energy than you use, here is information on how you can sell it to your energy supplier.

www.growyourownenergy.co.uk and **www.sunshinesolar.co.uk** Both sell solar panels, battery chargers, toys and garden products, plus all the wires and gismos.

www.windsave.com For domestic wind turbines.

Saving energy

We can all take some simple steps to reduce home energy use and save on emissions, fossil fuels and money.

Purchasing an energy-saving meter enables you to take a baseline measurement and observe the efficiencies that you are making. **www.ethicalsuperstore.com/category/eco-gadgets** has a couple of options.

Once you've established your baseline, carry out a domestic energy audit. Consider the structure of the building. Look at the roof and wall insulation, and draughts from windows and doors; could double glazing or draught protection strips be installed? Next look at your boiler; a new efficient boiler produces 10 per cent more heat per unit of energy than one bought even ten years ago, and savings of up to 70 per cent can be made. Explore the possibility of installing solar or wind technology in your home. Next, use the meter to judge the energy efficiency of your appliances and assess the impact of the various equipment you use. In all likelihood, the amount of wastage will shock your family and they will start turning off kit when not in use. Similarly with lighting; fit energy-efficient bulbs and watch the difference on the meter.

If you want inspiration, go to **www.theyellowhouse.org.uk** for an account of how an ordinary family has transformed a bog-standard terraced 1930s house into an energy-efficient eco-house.

Energy Saving Trust's ten point checklist

1. Turn your thermostat down. Reducing your room temperature by one degree Celcius could cut your heating bills by up to 10 per cent.

2. Is your water too hot? Your cylinder thermostat shouldn't need to be set higher than 60 degrees Celcius (140 degrees Fahrenheit).

3. Close your curtains at dusk to stop heat escaping through the windows.

4. Always turn off the lights when you leave a room.

5. Don't leave appliances on standby and remember not to leave appliances on charge unnecessarily.

6. If you're not filling up the washing machine, tumble dryer or dishwasher, use the half-load or economy programme.

7. Only boil as much water as you need (but remember to cover the elements if you're using an electric kettle).

8. A dripping hot water tap wastes energy and in one week wastes enough hot water to fill half a bath, so fix leaking taps and make sure they're fully turned off!

9. Use energy-saving light bulbs. Just one can save you £60 over the lifetime of the bulb – as they last up to 10 times longer than ordinary light bulbs.

10. Do a home energy check.

The following websites are full of simple ideas on how to reduce energy use and ideas for more radical changes.

www.energybulbs.co.uk or **www.thelightbulb.co.uk** For a wide range of energy-saving light bulbs. For information about low-energy light bulbs try this link: **www.nef.org.uk/energysaving/ lowenergylighting.htm**.

www.energysavingsecrets.co.uk Well over 100 articles written on the subject of energy, money and the environment, and they are adding new ones all the time. There is some quality material here.

www.energysavingtrust.org.uk/compare_and_buy_products A great resource to check before you buy an electrical item. Use the search facility to find the most efficient TV, fridge or washing machine in your price range. Also excellent for energy-saving ideas.

www.ethicalsuperstore.com/category/eco-gadgets Along with energy meters, this site offers a range of energy-saving devices, including the Bye Bye Standby plugs and remote controls that cut power to the devices when they're not in use, thus saving the power otherwise consumed.

www.excelfibre.com This company produces insulation made primarily from recycled newspapers, although this does need professional installation.

www.greenspec.co.uk The construction industry's definitive guide to building design, products, specification and construction, with a wealth of information on energy- and resource-efficient building materials and technologies.

www.homeinformationpacks.gov.uk Details about the Home Information Packs, including the Energy Performance Certificate, now compulsory with some house purchases.

www.livingroofs.org Keep warm in winter and cool in summer with a living roof, while encouraging wildlife.

www.nef.org.uk/actonCO2 The National Energy Foundation has a good section for individual consumers with practical suggestions.

www.pledgetodaysavetomorrow.co.uk Sign up and commit yourself to taking positive action in the home.

www.savaplug.co.uk or **www.shopeco.co.uk/savaplug-364-p.asp** Refrigeration is the single biggest user of energy in the home; this website sells a device that plugs into your fridge or freezer to reduce the amount of energy used to run the motor. Check for incompatibility on the website before you buy.

www.secondnatureuk.com For insulation products made from British wool.

www.sunspipe.co.uk Bring sunlight and/or ventilation into the building through a pipe in the roof; ideal for dark hallways, attic rooms and the workplace.

www.uk-energy-saving.com An all-round advice centre providing the necessary information to make sensible energy-saving choices. Covers a wide range of topics including energy-efficient boilers, light bulbs and insulation, as well as biothermal energy and switching to green electricity suppliers. The site has a blog and tips as well.

Energy blogs

Look at the high-quality blog at **http://howtosaveenergy. blogspot.com** or check out James Wilson's energy-related pages at **http://alt-e.blogspot.com**.

Embedded energy

Embedded energy is the energy consumed by all of the processes associated with the production of a product, from the acquisition of natural resources to product delivery. It complicates what might otherwise seem like simple choices and is easy to overlook in a rush of enthusiasm. For instance, does the embedded energy in a home wind turbine, made from steel and imported from China, actually represent a positive or negative contribution in terms of total carbon emissions? If a store uses thin, degradable, plastic bags, is this a better choice than recycled paper ones, whose bulk results in greater energy use for delivery? What about the comparable environmental impact of production and disposal?

Here are some useful sites:

en.wikipedia.org/wiki/Embodied_energy As happens with some of their articles, the neutrality of this article has been questioned; however, it remains a good introduction to the topic.

www.carbontrust.co.uk Has an interesting report to download called 'Carbon footprints in the supply chain: The next step for business'.

Batteries

Batteries contain heavy metals, many of which are toxic to people and the environment. They should not be thrown out with the rubbish but taken to the council waste management site for safe disposal.

The following sites contain handy info:

www.letsrecycle.com This provides information on the sorry state of British battery recycling and the EU perspective (0.5 per cent in the UK and 59 per cent in Belgium).

www.uniross.com/consumer_html/environment.php The manufacturers of rechargeable batteries have a downloadable factsheet, which explains the environmental benefits of rechargeable batteries, as well as a chart showing which batteries operate which equipment most effectively.

www.wrap.org.uk WRAP are trying to introduce battery recycling and are running several trials including a store take-back scheme. You can check on the site whether your authority is involved.

These suppliers have a good selection of batteries for cameras phones and general use, and provide a product matching guide to ensure you buy the correct battery:

www.batteriesplus.co.uk

www.batterylogic.co.uk

www.pentupenergy.co.uk

More information

If you need more information on the subject of green energy, **www.greenyearbook.org** provides categorised links.

Facts

- The production and use of energy is the leading source of humanity's greenhouse gas emissions.

- Fifteen centimetres (six inches) of loft insulation can save 20 per cent of energy costs.

- Cavity wall insulation reduces heat loss through walls by up to 60 per cent and could save as much as 40 per cent on heating bills.

- Using just one energy-saving light bulb could save you £5 a year.

- If every household installed one energy-saving bulb, the energy saved could power the lighting currently used in two million homes for a year.

- Lighting accounts for 20 per cent of the average household electricity bill.

- The average washing machine runs 274 cycles per year. A modern energy-efficient machine uses roughly one-third of the energy used by a regular machine. Washing clothes at 40 degrees uses one-third of the energy used to wash at 60 degrees. That's a lot of energy saved!

- The average household emits more carbon dioxide through energy use per year than the average car.

- Five billion batteries are sold in Europe each year, over 70 per cent of which end up in landfill.

- In the UK fossil fuels generate more than 70 per cent of our energy.

Rubbish

In 2005–6 each person in the UK generated an average of 512 kilograms (just over half a ton) of waste; they recycled 26 per cent of this. Most of the remaining waste goes to landfill, a disposal method that produces greenhouse gases, mainly carbon dioxide and methane. This is clearly not sustainable.

The mantra is simple: follow the three Rs – reduce, reuse, recycle. A good source of online information is **www.recycle-more.co.uk**, the 'one-stop recycling information centre'. Here you will find help and advice on all aspects of recycling at home, at school and in the workplace, including a list of the recycling symbols found on packaging and details of local facilities. For another all-round site try **www.wasteonline.org.uk**, where you'll find information sheets on how to deal with a wide range of objects and a searchable library. This site also covers the legislation appertaining to the waste industry.

Reduce

The advice is simple: first and foremost, buy only what you need; you'll save money too. Do your best to avoid being a victim of fads and fashions and 'must have' luxuries. Buy products that use the least packaging or recyclable packaging; in particular, avoid plastic-wrapped fruit and veg and only use plastic bags if really necessary. Take reusable bags with you when you shop. As a general rule, small local shops tend to use less packaging than large chains. There are some good tips on the American site **www.reduce.org**.

Approximately one-third of the food bought in the UK ends up in the bin; **www.lovefoodhatewaste.com** provides loads of information on buying and storing food and recipes for leftovers.

Go digital: read your newspapers and magazines online, and ask for e-mail correspondence and information whenever possible. And think before you print. Use envelope reuse labels; **www.treesforlife.org.uk/products/envelope_reuse_labels.html** has them.

Check out the news online

www.bbc.co.uk/news

www.dailymail.co.uk

www.fish4news.co.uk (local newspapers)

www.guardian.co.uk

www.independent.co.uk

www.thesun.co.uk

www.timesonline.co.uk

www.telegraph.co.uk

Buy reusable goods such as rechargeable batteries. Avoid disposable goods such as plastic cups, cameras and barbecues. Always consider repairing rather than replacing, in the first instance.

Choose non-toxic products whenever possible for things like pesticides, paints, solvents and household cleaners. Only throw empty containers in the general waste. **www.envocare.co.uk/hazardous_waste.htm** has information about the responsible disposal of toxic waste.

Stop junk mail

Save paper by removing your name from junk mailing lists. Send an email to the royal mail at **optout@royalmail.com**, giving your name and address. They will send you a form to enable you to opt out of unaddressed mail, such as mail addressed to 'the occupier'.

The Direct Mail Preference Scheme at **http://mpsonline.org.uk/mpsr** removes your name from commercial mailing lists to reduce unsolicited mail. It will not remove your name from companies that you have previously had an association with. You can pay a small fee for this service at **www.ItsMyPost.com** but be aware that you may stop receiving information and catalogues that you have previously requested.

Reuse

Don't throw away anything that can be reused such as plastic bags and glass containers. Plastic pots are ideal for seedlings and small plants, leftover bread can be given to the birds and old newspapers transformed into fire bricks (see the 'famous log maker' at **www.greenshop.co.uk**).

For more ideas:

www.junkk.com Look in their 'ideas' section, where you can share your good reuse ideas and pick up some tips from other contributors.

www.instructables.com This huge contributor site shows you how to do everything (most of which you really don't need to know); however, the 'green' section does have some extraordinary ideas.

www.recyclethis.co.uk This site is dedicated to thinking up creative ideas for reusing and recycling random stuff; you can browse the site for ideas or ask them to find a solution if you've got something you wish you could use.

Join a group such as Freecycle (**http://uk.freecycle.org**) or Don't Dump That (**www.dontdumpthat.com**). Both are free membership schemes that help you to direct perfectly usable items to someone in your area. Alternatively, sell unwanted stuff on **www.ebay.co.uk** or **www.preloved.co.uk**.

Recycle

Take full advantage of your local authority's recycling facilities, be they curbside collection or community recycling facilities (although if using the latter, try not to make a special journey). In most authorities it is easy to recycle glass, tins, cans and paper; however, they will recycle a wide range of goods.

www.recycle-more.co.uk To find out what you can recycle locally and where, type in your postcode and select 'bank locator' in the index. You can then select the item that you are trying to dispose of and the interactive map will show you the sites in your area that handle that type of waste. They also provide contact details for your local authority.

www.recyclenow.com Recycling facts and information with an interactive map for locating local recycling facilities. Part of **www.wrap.org.uk**, the Waste and Resources Action Programme, which works to increase the use of recycled materials.

www.recycledproducts.org.uk Provides a national, comprehensive database of products made from recycled materials – everything from sports equipment to animal bedding to coffins.

www.recycling-guide.org.uk Has a complete list of items that can be recycled and how. Good general information.

Compost

Use a compost bin for uncooked vegetables and fruit, cardboard and garden waste. Good instructions can be found at **www.homecomposting.org.uk**. For more information see the 'Gardening' section on page 88.

Donate to charity

High street shops will take saleable clothing, household goods, gifts, books and CDs. **www.charityshops.org.uk/locator.php** will provide local contact details. Spectacles, furniture, printer cartridges, mobile phones and computers can be given via more specialist charities.

Bikes

www.re-cycle.org Will ship your unwanted bikes to Africa.

Binoculars

www.worldlandtrust.org Will take binoculars and other wildlife-related material.

Books

www.bookaid.org Will send books to places where they are scarce.

www.greenmetropolis.com Lists the books you want to sell. There's a huge selection for sale.

CDs, DVDs, CDRs, VHS and cassette tapes
www.thelaundry.biz/cds Mail them your unwanted CDs and the like and they will extract the polycarbonate and aluminimum content – this is important as they are nearly indestructible and will sit forever in landfill. Alternatively, auction them on **http://onlyonepound.org** to raise money for Wateraid and Sightsavers.

Computers

www.computeraid.org and **www.computersforcharities.co.uk** Both promise to destroy all your personal data before donating computers and similar items to developing countries.

www.itforcharities.co.uk Provides a comprehensive listing of UK organisations that will reuse computers and related technology.

Curtains
www.thecurtainexchange.net/secondhand.htm Will sell your unwanted curtains in their shops provided they are in good condition. Unsold curtains are donated to charity.

Electrical and white goods
www.recyclenow.com Use the 'where can I recycle' to find your local recycling point. Manufacturers by law now have responsibility for their products throughout their lifecycles. This means that take-back and collection schemes for obsolete products should be offered by the retailer; ask about their schemes when purchasing new goods.

www.weeeman.org Information and advice on the disposal of waste electrical and electronic equipment.

Foreign currency
www.helptheaged.org.uk This, and other high street charities, will relieve you of unwanted hard currency.

Furniture
www.crispej.org.uk The place for the recycling of office furniture and computers.

www.frn.org.uk A network of local organisations that will channel unwanted furniture and electrical goods to people in need.

Hearing aids
www.oxfordhearingcentre.co.uk Donate old hearing aids to hearing-impaired children in Romania.

Hazardous materials
www.recycle-more.co.uk Don't dump it in the general waste; contact your local authority for advice via this site.

Mobiles
www.recyclemymobile.co.uk Will buy mobiles in good condition. For a more altruistic approach try **www.recyclingappeal.com**, which supports a wide range of charities, or **www.fones4schools.co.uk**. The site **www.fonebak.com** has information about retail outlets that will take back old mobile phones.

Oil
www.oilbankline.org.uk Find your nearest oil bank for waste engine oil.

Paint
www.communityrepaint.org.uk Locates your nearest donation centre and passes paint on to community and voluntary groups, or disposes of it responsibly at a recycling centre.

Printer cartridges
www.recyclingappeal.com and **www.cartridges4charity.co.uk** Both support a number of charities.

Spectacles
www.secondsightproject.com and **www.vao.org.uk/spectacles** Find opticians who collect unwanted spectacles and donate them to the Third World.

Tools
www.tfsr.org Tools for Self Reliance works to sends tools to Africa. Send them an email to arrange collection.

Vehicles
www.mvda.org.uk/memberssearch.aspx For responsible end-of-life vehicle disposal. They will also help you find used spare parts.

Wood
www.recyclewood.org.uk Find your nearest wood recycling facility. They also sell recycled wood products.

Warning

When a plastic bag purports to be 'degradable' it does not mean biodegradable – a degradable carrier bag does not compost, it simply degrades faster than normal plastic bags.

Look out for new maize-based compostable packaging, but be sure to compost this or put it with food waste; it will contaminate recyclable plastic waste.

Plastic

Plastic waste is clogging up the world. Wherever you travel you see mashed up plastic waste in drainage systems, rivers and roadsides, and hanging as 'grannies knickers' in the trees. More harm still is being done to the oceans, where plastic is being consumed by marine creatures, often with fatal effects.

These sites give you the low-down.

http://news.bbc.co.uk/2/hi/science/nature/6218698.stm An article on how plastic is poisoning the oceans.

www.belu.org Use biodegradable water bottles made from corn-starch.

www.cynarplc.com A vision for the future? A company planning to 'recover synthetic fuel from a variety of used plastic sources'.

www.fakeplasticfish.com One woman's quest to eliminate plastic.

A blog with loads of links and thoughts about plastic and how to avoid it.

www.wasteonline.org.uk/resources/InformationSheets/Plastics. htm A good introduction to the problems of plastic waste.

Facts

- Every two hours the UK throws out sufficient rubbish to fill the Albert Hall.

- The energy saving from recycling one bottle will power a 100-watt light bulb for almost an hour or power a computer for 20 minutes.

- Around 56 per cent of all plastics waste is used packaging; three-quarters of this is from households.

- Up to 60 per cent of the rubbish that ends up in the dustbin could be recycled.

- One in three bags of food purchased ends up in the rubbish. The carbon cost of this is the equivalent of taking one in five cars off the road.

- Only 7 per cent of plastic is recycled in the UK.

- The UK produces 5.2 million tons of hazardous waste each year, of which only 40 per cent is recycled or treated, while 39 per cent goes to landfill.

- An estimated 1.8 tons of oil are saved for every ton of recycled polythene produced.

- It takes just 25 two-litre plastic pop bottles to make one adult-size fleece jacket.

- In the UK we use 15 million plastic bottles a day.

- An estimated 17.5 billion plastic bags are given away by super-markets annually. That is 290 bags for every person in the UK.

- **The amount of paper thrown out annually equates to four kilograms of waste paper per household in the UK per week.**

- **Babies' nappies account for about 2 per cent of household rubbish. This is equivalent to the weight of nearly 70,000 double-decker buses every year. If lined up, these buses would stretch from London to Edinburgh.**

Home improvement and construction

Many greening home improvements are related to saving energy, which is covered on page 50. This is where information regarding insulation, energy-saving boilers and appliances is to be found. Information on home plumbing is in the 'Water' section on page 84, while chemicals in the home are discussed on page 78.

Renovation materials

www.aecb.net On the Sustainable Building Association site look under 'information' for some well-written factsheets on sustainable renovation and maintenance, including building and health-related issues.

www.eco-renovation.org Newly launched when we visited, so the links and associated businesses listed here were limited. The aim is for the site to become a source of information about how to make existing homes more sustainable and to facilitate local networks. You can sign up for their newsletter.

www.greenspec.co.uk Has all the information on all the materials that you are likely to need. They also list a wide selection of manufacturers for the different products; unfortunately, they are not set as hyperlinks.

www.thehouseplanner.co.uk A comprehensive set of links, well-categorised and detailed – if you can't find it here, it probably doesn't exist.

Suppliers

www.constructionresources.com High-performance building materials and associated systems that have been selected because they use safe, renewable, natural materials. They are concerned that products are energy efficient and keep to a minimum the use of non-renewable and non-recyclable resources. Includes floor coverings and paints.

www.ecomerchant.co.uk An environmentally conscious builder's merchant with lots of product information and choice.

www.greenbuildingstore.co.uk For building materials, household fittings and a range of natural paints.

www.oldhousestore.co.uk Traditional and ecological materials for restoring and maintaining an old house.

www.reclaimbuildingsupply.com For a county-by-county list of dealers in reclaimed fixtures, fittings and building materials.

www.safeguardeurope.com Specialises in damp-proofing and waterproofing solutions and supplies. There are downloadable datasheets on a wide range of topics and product details, but note that they are not necessarily green.

www.salvo.co.uk A searchable directory of architectural salvage merchants; someone out there should have what you are looking for.

www.wow-wow.co.uk A bright and freshly designed site selling paints, oils, lighting, insulation, heating, solar-powered lighting and equipment, and many other products for the home.

Painting and decorating

Most paints are made from petrochemicals, using large quantities of embedded energy and ultimately resulting in toxic waste. Modern eco-paint alternatives now come in a spectrum of colours and give a durable and attractive finish. The eco paints tend to be of a more sloppy texture and are porous, unlike conventional paints, which create a plastic film on the walls.

There is concern that the quantities of titanium dioxide that are being used in the paint industry (also in paper and detergent manufacture) are leading to a world shortage. This substance is mined and demand is leading to the opening of new mines in pristine habitats. Titanium dioxide is used in many eco and natural paints, although some manufacturers select theirs from carefully monitored mines.

To investigate the issues further go to **http://ec.europa.eu/dgs/jrc**, the European Commission Joint Research Centre, where their reports on such things as solvent toxicity are published. Use the search engine to find the subject of interest.

There are a number of companies making natural or eco paints. Here are a few to start off with:

www.earthbornpaints.co.uk An extensive range of paints, varnishes and associated products including a clay and casein paint as well as glazes and pigments. Available from a number of stockists listed on the site.

www.ecoartisan.org A London-based decorating and design company that gives advice on the uses of natural paints and discusses the technical issues.

www.ecospaints.com As well as 108 colours and a wide range of paint finishes, there is a range of woodstains, floor paints, radiator paint, wood glue, plaster sealer and similar products. They also provide a colour-matching service, and a free white matchpot and paint sample for you to feel and see. Order from the website and they will deliver the next day.

www.nutshellpaints.co.uk A range of 100 per cent ecological paints. They suggest you purchase a specifier kit to select your colour (the value of this is deducted from your first order). Order online.

Dispose of old paint

Give to a good cause at **www.communityrepaint.org.uk**.

Wall and floor coverings

There are limited options for eco wallpaper where the environmental issues are centred around ink discharge and disposal, strong odour emission and, of course, the use of paper from sustainable sources. Eco-friendly floor coverings are more plentiful.

Wallpaper

www.ecocentric.co.uk A small range of eco wallpapers and paints by designer Oliver Heath.

www.grahambrown.com This company has introduced a small selection of wallpapers printed with water-based ink on sustainable paper.

www.next.co.uk Their wallpaper is sourced from renewable, sustainable forests. They make no claims for their inks.

Flooring

www.alternativeflooring.com For natural fibre floor covering and wool carpets.

www.concept-carpet.co.uk Jacob wool carpets dyed with natural colourings and with jute backings.

www.interfloor.com For rubber underlay made from recycled materials.

www.onevillage.co.uk Supply a range of ethically sourced, artisan-made rugs and coir flooring.

www.rugmark.org Make sure that the rug you buy has not been made by exploited children.

www.ryburnrubber.co.uk Reuse old car tyres to make a range of

Terrazzo floor tiles, suitable for home use as well as block paving, play and leisure floors.

www.sustainablefloors.co.uk All the information you need to understand the environmental impact of your choice of flooring.

www.urbanliving.co.uk For a lovely range of hand-woven flooring, wallpaper made from natural products, recycled glass tiles and wooden worktops. They also sell Marmoleum, a natural product that resembles vinyl flooring but is more sustainable, and Nutshell paints.

Wood

Wood is a sound environmental product, providing its provenance is sound. To make sure that you are not contributing to the destruction of ancient forests, only buy wood that is certified by the Forestry Stewardship Council (**www.fsc-uk.org**). The timber will either have the FSC logo or your receipt will show a Chain of Custody (COC) number. The other certification authority is the Programme for the Endorsement of Forest Certification (**www.pefc.co.uk**). If the wood is from a UK source it may be certified by either of these schemes, which work to the UK Woodland Assurance Standard (**www.ukwas.org.uk**).

When it comes to treating, preserving and staining wood, many of the paint suppliers listed earlier have products in their ranges. Also check out **www.safeguardeurope.com/applications/wood_preservation.php** for downloadable datasheets on wood rot and woodworm, and **www.greenspec.co.uk** for information about finishes.

Other woody sites:

www.foe.co.uk or **www.greenpeace.org.uk** Search either site under 'wood' for their lists of good and bad woods.

www.recyclewood.org.uk Whether you want to buy recycled wood, or dispose of it, this site will assist you in finding a local facility.

www.recycle-it.org The Timber Recycling Information Centre 'aims to encourage, inform, and enable users and specifiers of timber to reduce the amount of timber in the waste stream and to implement more sustainable waste management practices'.

www.trada.co.uk Look under 'technical information' for a wide selection of factsheets on wood-related themes and detailed information on over 100 varieties of timber. Software for design, detailed drawings and a good deal more are available to members.

Eco building construction

If you are in the fortunate position of building your own green home, there is a wealth of sites to help. A good one to start with is **www.thehouseplanner.co.uk**, which has a huge number of links – everything from inspiration, architects and regulations to the materials that you will need and furniture.

http://sustainabledevelopments.net A directory site that would be invaluable to anyone thinking of a self-build project; includes links on sustainable homes, the solar-powered house, green design and eco construction.

www.aecb.net Provides a number of useful factsheets and articles.

www.cat.org.uk The Centre for Alternative Technology is a great resource for the self-builder.

www.ebuild.co.uk Everything the self-builder could need to know is here, simply outlined with a huge amount of back-up information. Be aware that the site does not pretend to be a source of green information.

www.gaiagroup.org A Scottish-based site comprising three companies with a shared ecological vision. You can find some good inspiration and information here.

www.netregs.gov.uk You need to know the regs!

www.selfbuildabc.co.uk/building/green-self-build-home.asp Has good starter information for anyone considering a self-build project. The site can also provide help in finding plots for sale.

Facts

● **The handmade carpet industry exploits around 300,000 children.**

● **The merbau tree, which grows to 100 feet in the forests of New Guinea, will be commercially extinct in 35 years at legal rates of logging, earlier with the illegal trade.**

● **Since the 1950s the volume of chemicals in general use has gone up 35 times; there are now more than 15,000 chemicals in circulation.**

● **Twenty per cent of paint purchased goes unused.**

● **A new self-build home is zero-rated for VAT.**

● **Between 18 and 20 per cent of homes completed annually are self-build projects.**

Furniture, soft-furnishings and homewares

The reuse and recycle mantra comes in again when it comes to furniture. There is a massive amount of second-hand furniture, much of it in excellent condition, on the internet. Of course, there is eBay, and then there are also local swap site schemes such as **http://uk.freecycle.org** or **www.dontdumpthat.com**. The furniture reuse network **www.frn.org.uk** is also promising a sale page on their site soon.

However, if it is new that you are looking for, the following all use recycled or certified wood and natural organic or Fairtrade materials. If you are using a high street store, or shopping online, then check out the wood certification schemes on page 71 before you shop. John Lewis (**www.johnlewis.com**), for instance, will guarantee the provenance of its own brand lines, while Ikea (**www.ikea.com**) will not accept wood that is 'illegally logged or comes from intact natural forests' and in the long term is aiming for 100 per cent certified woods. Habitat (**www.habitat.co.uk**) works with the TFT (Tropical Forestry Trust) to ensure that all of its teak furniture products are compliant, and with FSC (Forest Stewardship Council) to ensure full certification across the range in the coming years.

Mainly for living spaces

www.arborvetum.co.uk Dining room, living room and conservatory furniture made from certified and recycled wood.

www.namaste-uk.com A small range of Fairtrade furniture made from recycled teak.

www.organic-furnishings.co.uk An eco-aware upholsterer that uses Earth-friendly materials to make upholstered chairs, cushions, throws and fabrics. They promise some more furniture to come soon.

www.reestore.com This company 'takes everyday waste objects and cheekily turns them into charming yet functional pieces of furniture and accessories'. This includes the shopping trolley chair and the wash drum table.

Mainly for bedrooms

www.naturalhome-products.com Natural and organic mattresses, bed linen and nursery goods. The company avoids using chemicals, so the products are particularly suitable for allergy sufferers.

www.warrenevans.com Beds and bedroom furniture made from Fairtrade, sustainably sourced wood and organic mattresses are on offer here. The lines are simple and contemporary and products are all made by hand using traditional joinery techniques.

For the whole home

www.benchmark-furniture.com With a long track record of sustainable production and high-quality craftsmanship, this company produces 'contemporary classics' and has an impressive showroom on the site. One of their designers is Terence Conran.

www.oneecohome.co.uk Modern, stylised furniture and accessories for the entire home. The range is not large, but all the products are beautifully designed.

www.untothislast.co.uk Innovative design and stunning structures characterise the furniture made by this workshop. The wood comes from sustainable forests and the finishes are of wax and oil.

Furniture directory

For links to furniture makers using sustainable or recycled raw materials, check out **www.thehouseplanner.co.uk/ furniture.html**.

Soft furnishings, accessories and gifts

http://onevillage.org Supports cooperatives in the developing world. Has a selection of duvet covers, throws, cushions and wide range of home accessories. There are also rugs and flooring.

www.ecocentric.co.uk A wide range of contemporary accessories for the home including eating and drinking (plates, bowls and tableware, glassware and utensils); living and sleeping (mattresses, cushions, throws and candles); and lighting, bathroom and energy-saving goods.

www.ecological-living.co.uk An assemblage of stylish natural and ethically sourced products including kitchen, glassware and lighting.

www.ethicalonestopshop.com Look under house and home for a wide selection of ethically produced homewares.

www.lazye.co.uk The Lazy Environmentalist has a chic site with a limited choice of high-quality, environmentally friendly homewares.

www.lumadirect.com Organic cotton linens, blankets, throws and cushions.

www.phoenixwoodcrafts.co.uk A fabulous collection of hand-crafted bowls, lamps and utensils all crafted from recycled wood. The outdoor thrones are extraordinary.

www.tactile-interiors.co.uk Eco-friendly accessories for the home. The green glassware, black bamboo bowls and biodegradable plastic plates are particularly attractive.

Facts

● **Twenty-five per cent of the pesticides used globally are used in the production of textiles.**

● **A study commissioned by UK Timber Trade Federation reported that 56 per cent of all wood and wood products imported into the UK in 2005 were certified.**

● **The EU estimates that 80 per cent of the wood imported from Brazil is illegally produced; Indonesia 73 per cent and Cameroon 50 per cent.**

● **Sixty-two per cent of tropical imports to the UK could potentially come from illegal sources.**

Home cleaning and laundry

There is a great deal of commercial pressure on us to keep our homes immaculately clean using an ever-increasing selection of products specially designed to meet every conceivable need. There is some evidence to suggest that living such sterile lives may be bad for our health and might play a part in the increase in childhood allergies. We do have other options. Commercial green cleaning products are non-toxic and less harmful to the environment and are now readily available.

Products you may have around the house such as lemons, vinegar and bicarbonate of soda are traditional cleaners and they may be cheaper too. There is, however, an argument against extending this use for lemons. It is suggested that growing lemons for cleaning would take land away from farming for food, and it requires international transportation and high pesticide use (unless using organic lemons). It is one of those environmental no-win situations, so discerning use of lemons is called for!

Buy:

- products in the largest containers

- the strongest concentrations possible (transfer products into a smaller container and dilute to prevent unintentional overuse)

- recycled kitchen and loo paper.

Avoid:

- aerosols

- special products for every room

- using anything showing the dangerous chemical symbol, except as a last resort.

For a run-through of the basic advice watch the introductory video on **www.videojug.com/film/how-to-clean-your-house-the-eco-friendly-way**. The site has a selection of other cleaning videos you can watch too.

For further information, check out these sites:

www.channel4.com/4homes/style/eco_cleaning-2.html For a list of tips and hints.

www.newdream.org/newsletter/greencleaning.php Some good information from this American site.

Eco manufacturers

www.biodegradable.biz Bio D products

www.ecover.com Ecover

www.ifyoucare.com Unbleached paper and recycled aluminium products

www.faithinnature.co.uk Clear Spring products

www.simplegreen.co.uk Simple Green products

Dishwashing

The dishwasher versus hand-washing debate. Don't forget, if considering purchasing a new machine use the Energy Saving Trust's comparison site **www.energysavingtrust.org.uk/compare_ and_buy_products**.

http://environment.about.com/od/greenlivingdesign/a/dishwashers. htm Has a detailed discussion plus links to articles on how to load your dishwasher efficiently and buying tips.

www.whatprice.co.uk/environmental/save-water.html For the low-down on dishwashing.

Chemicals and toxicity

www.epa.gov/kidshometour Designed for kids, so they can understand the chemicals in the home, but good for adults who want to learn more about the products in the cupboard, how to use them safely and what to do in case of an accident.

www.ewg.org/chemindex The Environmental Working Group provides news and research items on each individual chemical type, the related health risks and the routes of exposure.

www.foe.co.uk/resource/briefings/risky_chemicals_in_the_home.p df This material is now dated, but it does contain a list of chemicals to avoid. See also the related factsheet **www.foe.co.uk/ resource/factsheets/chemicals_and_your_health.html**.

www.healthy-house.co.uk A site for people suffering from allergies and chemical sensitivity with a huge range of natural products to help sufferers, including dust-mite-proof bedding, cotton and silk clothing, humidifiers, mould allergy products, allergy tests, and a huge amount more.

www.wwf.org.uk/chemicals The results of the World Wildlife Fund's campaign against hazardous chemicals. Look under 'your home' for a room-by-room breakdown on substances to avoid.

Laundry

The basic eco advice is simple and works well for most washes. However, when it comes to a grass-stained, mud-encrusted rugby kit or greasy, wine-splattered tablecloths, the chances are that eco washing doesn't cut the mustard. The sites below will solve all your laundry dilemmas but be aware that some of the advice does call for solvents and petrochemical-based products.

Basic eco advice

- Wash at 30 degrees.

- Use biodegradable, environmentally friendly washing detergent.

- Try using Eco Balls* and dispense with detergent altogether.

- When your machine dies, replace with an A- or A*-rated machine.

- Don't use a dryer.

*Eco or Aqua Balls work by ionising the water and encouraging sweat and other water soluble molecules to lift off the fabric. Some people love 'em; others are more sceptical.

---

http://home.stonehavenlife.com/greenhome/stainclean.html
A simple listing of stains and eco solutions. You'll need a supply of milk, vinegar, cornflour, bicarbonate of soda and unseasoned meat tenderiser (for urine stains!). **http://home.howstuffworks.com/laundry-tips.htm**.

www.goodhousekeeping.co.uk Always reliable, *Good Housekeeping Magazine* has a fantastic forum where you can ask your unresolved questions.

www.housekeeping.about.com/cs/laundry A comprehensive advice site covering washing tips, stain removal and disaster recovery. There are plentiful links to external sites.

www.laundry-alternative.com An odd site and very US-orientated but contains some unusual articles, including one on the chemical analysis of commercial detergent, bacteria and viruses in the wash and a quantum approach to the problem of the missing socks.

The following are good web shops for eco laundry and home cleaning products:

www.eco-essentials.co.uk

www.ecotopia.co.uk

www.ethicalsuperstore.com

www.greenshop.co.uk

www.soorganic.com

www.ecozone.co.uk

Make your own detergent

Feeling creative? Go to **www.recipezaar.com/70088** and learn how to cook up your own washing detergent.

Washing machines and dryers

These sites help you to decide which machine is best for you and the environment. The washing machine is seen as a necessity but both its water and energy consumption must be considered and both vary considerably from machine to machine, as does washing efficiency. A tumble dryer is optional and is one of the most energy-hungry pieces of equipment in the home (and top of the environmentalists' hit list). Most tumble dryers have an energy C rating but the energy use within this category varies by about one-third, so it is worth doing the research before you buy. A-rated machines are just becoming available, but are more expensive.

www.energysavingtrust.org.uk/compare_and_buy_products A product comparison facility that enables you to select the most efficient machine (washer, dryer or dishwasher) in your price range.

www.greenandeasy.co.uk Under 'information' lists a number of the better washing machines in terms of energy efficiency.

www.nef.org.uk/energyadvice/washing.htm A serious look at washing machine energy consumption. There is a chart that compares energy use at the various temperatures for machines in the various energy rating categories (A–F).

www.washerhelp.co.uk A really useful site for detailed information about washing machines, including a forum with a section entitled 'environmental issues and the washing machine' for discussion on water consumption, air drying and disposal of old machines. They supply useful information about the efficiency of various types of detergent in machines and the thorny problem of limescale build-up.

Maximise dryer efficency

- Spin clothes as fast as possible before drying.

- Fill to the maximum load.

- Regularly clean filters.

- Fit in a well-ventilated location.

The pitfalls

Be aware that low-temperature washing leaves residues in your machine that will eventually damage the machine and stain the wash – one site recommends running half a cup of bicarbonate of soda through the machine monthly to avoid this. Another worry is that low-temperature washing does not remove allergens – if these cause health problems in your family, then this style of washing is not for you.

In the news

Read 'Allergy fear on "green" laundry' at **http://news.bbc. co.uk/1/hi/health/6669551.stm**.

Drying naturally

Line drying is the most environmental option, but, of course, it is not reliable in our rainy climate and is unavailable to flat dwellers. These websites might help:

www.dpcompany.co.uk For a traditional wooden SheilaMaid, clothes horses and clothes lines.

www.ecowashinglines.co.uk A good selection of indoor and outdoor drying lines and airers with installation guides and videos.

Dry cleaning

The nasty ingredient that goes into dry cleaning fluid is perchloroethylene (perc) which produces the eye-watering smell characteristic of dry cleaners. Not only does it raise concerns about the health impacts of those who work with it, but it is toxic to the environment if it is not disposed of correctly. There is an alternative called GreenEarth dry cleaning, which uses siloxane and has been adopted by some of the biggest names in the business. So if you have to use a dry cleaner, choose one that uses this product.

www.greenearth.co.uk For information on GreenEarth dry cleaning products. They have a search system to enable you to find your nearest cleaner.

www.johnsoncleaners.co.uk With 520 stores nationwide (including Sketchleys) you should be able to find one in your area. They are not all using GreenEarth, but are in the process of making the transition.

Facts

- **The average washing machines runs 274 cycles per year.**

- **Ninety per cent of the machine's energy use goes on heating the water.**

- **Twelve per cent of domestic water goes on the laundry.**

- **Three hundred man-made chemicals have been detected in the human body.**

- **The strongest concentrations of chemicals found in the body are in breast milk.**

- **Switching from 40 to 30 degree washes saves a further 40 per cent in energy cost.**

- **Rinsing clothes three or four times in cold water after washing at 30 degrees produces results comparable with a hotter wash.**

- **A half-load does not use half the energy or half the water.**

- **Not using a tumble dryer and line drying instead is a 100 per cent energy-saving solution.**

- **Dryer balls are non-toxic and environmentally friendly; they can reduce drying time by 25 per cent, and avoid the need for fabric softeners.**

Water

During spells of hot dry weather it is natural to think about ways of saving water, but the changes in rainfall patterns over the past few years have left many with water restrictions imposed by their water suppliers through the winter too. It is not just the water that you save when you take action – the embedded energy that is used in the water purification process is saved too, so reducing domestic consumption is good for reducing carbon emissions as well.

For information on using water for laundry and dishwashing, see page 76.

General information

www.cat.org.uk Look under 'free information service' for basic information sheets on grey water, rainwater harvesting, composting toilets, water filter, pumps and small scale sewerage treatment. If this is not sufficient there are factsheets to download, for a nominal fee, and a more substantial booklet that you can buy. They also sell rainbutts, diversion kits and other associated products in their store.

www.environment-agency.gov.uk/subjects/waterres/287169 The Environment Agency's water pages have information promoting water meters and advice on the prudent use of water, rainwater harvesting and grey water. There is a great deal of information on the site for both domestic and business users. For a slightly more detailed practical approach look under 'energy and water saving' on another government site: **www.direct.gov.uk/en/Environmentandgreenerliving**.

www.waterfootprint.org This site says, 'The water footprint is an indicator of water use that looks at the direct and indirect water use of a consumer or producer.' It takes the subject to a national level as it is sponsored by the UN. There are quick and extensive individual water footprint calculators.

www.waterwise.org.uk A non-profit organisation dedicated to reducing water wastage in the UK. They work with water companies, the government and the business community to become more efficient with water. There is excellent information for the domestic consumer, including somewhat fey video presentations, but more interesting is the material on embedded water. Water hidden in our food and drink we might consider, but apparently 30.6 per cent of water use is embedded in industrial goods such as cars, bikes and TVs.

The international dimension

www.noaa.gov The US National Oceanic and Atmospheric Administration is the world's largest archive of climate, geophysical and environmental, and global oceanographic data. The site has good information on satellites.

www.unesco.org/water UNESCO's portal aims to improve access to information about freshwater. There are details of the programmes they run and the global issues surrounding access to fresh water. There are links to other water-related programmes, and a good dictionary of hydrology is included.

www.wateraid.org/uk For information about their campaign to provide water, sanitation and hygiene education to people in developing countries.

The real cost of a bag of salad

Take a look at this article from the *Independent*: **http://www. independent.co.uk/environment/the-real-cost-of-a-bag-of-salad-you-pay-99p-africa-pays-50-litres-of-fresh-water-476030.html**.

Reducing domestic consumption

There are a number of products that you can install that will help reduce your water consumption. A good starting point is **http://www.greenbuildingstore.co.uk/water.php** for water-saving collection advice and case studies. The site offers a wide range of devices from taps and flow reducers to waterless urinals. They also do a neat wall-mounted water butt that is attached to the exterior water supply.

www.droughtbuster.co.uk This site sells a syphon pump that moves water from your water butt, bath, shower or sink to your garden.

www.hippo-the-watersaver.co.uk To reduce water consumption in the cistern, a hippo is a heavy gauge polyethylene package, which opens up, origami style, into an open-ended box shape when installed. This reduces the amount of water used in each flush in cisterns fitted prior to the reduction in capacity in 2001.

www.save-a-flush.co.uk A cistern water-saving device that claims to save around a litre a flush.

www.tapmagic.co.uk Offers a range of water-saving tap inserts that work with existing taps and save up to 70 per cent.

A–Z of water-saving tips

Browse **http://news.bbc.co.uk/1/hi/world/2945018.stm**.

Composting toilets

www.compostingtoilet.org An American site with a mission to facilitate the use of composting toilets with some interesting information on the subject.

www.elementalsolutions.co.uk Compost toilets, toilets flushed by rainwater, and chemical and water-free urinals.

www.jenkinspublishing.com/humanure.html Featuring free downloadable copies of older versions of this American enthusiast's book *Humanure*, a photo gallery, instruction manuals and much more.

www.lowimpact.org/topics_compost_toilets.htm Provides introductory information, details of courses, a printable factsheet and a forum where you can check your facts with those in the know.

www.natsol.co.uk Composting toilets for places without mains supply.

www.stewardwood.org For information on treebogs and how to build one.

Gardening

(See also the 'Gardening' section on page 88.)

www.cambridge-water.co.uk/about_you/save_garden.asp Offers advice on the efficient use of water in the garden.

www.solarflow-garden.co.uk Offers an automated irrigation system using the power of the sun and any available water source that will operate even in cloudy conditions. They also sell water butts.

Recycling and rainwater harvesting

www.freerain.co.uk Sells several systems for the home and garden as well as larger settings.

www.rainharvesting.co.uk A company that has innovative products for domestic, garden and commercial purposes.

www.reducewaterbills.co.uk A personal site from a man who set out to reduce his consumption with a simple rainwater-capture system, suitable for the average DIYer.

www.ukrha.org The Rainwater Harvesting Association promotes this activity using large tanks buried in the garden.

Reed beds

www.cresswater.co.uk A company specialising in reed bed construction with some nice illustrations on how the process works.

www.envirowise.gov.uk/166746 Good introductory material on reed beds and how they work.

www.yes-reedbeds.co.uk They supply domestic, agricultural and industrial reed beds. They suggest that a four-metre-squared reed bed would work for a family of four to six people.

Facts

- **A shower running at mains pressure uses around 20 litres of water per minute.**

- **A loo fitted before 1991 probably has a cistern capacity of 9 litres; one fitted between 1992 and 2001 has a 7.5-litre capacity; and one from 2001 takes 6 litres.**

- **If the adult population turned off the tap while brushing their teeth, 180 million gallons of water would be saved daily.**

- **England has far less available water per person per year than France, Italy or even Spain: England has 1,334 cubic metres per person a year; France 3,065 cubic metres; Italy 2785 cubic metres; and Spain 2,775 cubic metres.**

- **We use nearly double the amount of water today than we did 25 years ago.**

- **One kilogram of beef requires 16,000 litres of water to grow.**

Gardening

For many people, the garden is a little bit of nature within their reach, and there has been an increase of interest in the topic largely fuelled by inspirational TV gardeners. The basic environmental issues are around pesticide and herbicide use, the over-reliance on peat-based products, water usage and the increased use of environmentally unfriendly equipment and accessories, including patio heaters, barbecues and some garden furniture.

The best environmental solution is, of course, to go organic. However, in this section some non-organic sites have been covered as they do provide good information and choice for those who are not yet ready to make that commitment.

General gardening sites and shops

www.bbc.co.uk/gardening Although this is not a specialist green site, there is a huge amount of relevant information on this well-presented site. They have sections on organic gardening, creating a wildflower meadow and wildlife gardening. There is also a great pest and disease identifier.

www.greengardener.co.uk Specialists in biological and organic pest control and wormeries. They also have an excellent selection of insect houses, bird feeders and live bird food to promote biodiversity in your garden.

www.gardenorganic.org.uk This site from the Henry Doubleday Research Association is probably the best one-stop site on organic gardening. There are full guidelines on organic gardening and a handy 'what to do in the garden this month' section. The catalogue for their online garden centre, with a full range of products, is found at **www.organiccatalog.com**.

www.just-green.com Everything you could want for your garden barring the plants, although they do have a limited selection of fruit trees, carnivorous plants and seed mixes.

www.originalorganics.co.uk Very good on wormeries, and the site also has water butts, garden solar lighting and galvanised buckets.

www.rhs.org.uk In their 'advice' section the Royal Horticultural Society website has a good range of factsheets on conservation and the environment. There is also information on vegetable growing and a fantastic plant finder.

Grow your own

Here's a good read for anyone interested in getting the kids involved in the garden: **www.thekidsgarden.co.uk/OrganicGardening.html**.

Organic plants and seeds

www.chilternseeds.co.uk Some 4,500 seeds to choose from, many of which are rare, heirloom or unusual, and including organic vegetables.

www.plantconnection.co.uk and **www.kingsplants.co.uk** Both have organic herb and vegetable plants, although the flowering plants on the sites are not organic.

www.secretseeds.com A wonderful collection of seeds, but only some of the vegetable and herb seeds are organic. Also supplies seeds for green manures, ancient grains, wildflowers and grasses, plus a unusual selection of decorative plants.

www.suttons.co.uk Features Alan Titchmarsh's range of organic vegetables amongst the huge range.

Biodiversity

www.bgci.org Information about plant conservation from Botanic Gardens Conservation International.

www.kew.org There is some really interesting work going on at Kew and it's well worth browsing their site.

www.nhm.ac.uk/nature-online/life/plants-fungi/postcode-plants/ search.html A horrid URL but home to the Natural History Museum's native plant database. Type in your postcode and find out about plants that are indigenous to your area, and whether or not they are garden-worthy.

www.wigglywigglers.co.uk Written by a farmer with regular blog updates on what's going on in the fields, there is also an online shop specialising in wildlife products for the garden. If you want to attract wildlife into your garden, you can find a home for them here. You also can stock your pond and buy plants, composters and English-grown flowers.

www.wildaboutgardens.org You'll find information, a forum and blogs at this interactive site, set up by the Royal Horticultural

Society in conjunction with the Wildlife Trust. The aim is to encourage people to see their gardens as nature reserves and to enjoy and share the experience.

www.wildlife-gardening.co.uk Jenny Steel's personal website is a celebration of the wildlife in her garden and a great resource for others who would like to follow suit.

www.wildlife-gardening.org.uk Another excellent site aimed at gardeners who want to actively encourage wildlife, with a range of interesting feature articles, a diary and news.

Online stores supplying wildflowers and seeds

www.meadowmania.co.uk

www.wildflowers.co.uk

www.wildflower.org.uk

www.wildseeds.co.uk

Pesticides and herbicides

www.beyondpesticides.org Look under 'info services' on this American site for good information on how to treat pests through the understanding of their habitat and how to prevent further invasions. There is also a huge amount of material on the pesticides themselves and the hazards that they pose.

www.epa.gov/pesticides/index.htm The US Environmental Protection Agency's pesticide section is a superb resource if you want to investigate pesticides in some detail. It includes information on the different types of pesticides and factsheets on specific chemicals as well as ecological considerations.

www.pan-uk.org Website of the Pesticide Action Network, which is working to eliminate the hazards associated with pesticides.

www.pesticides.gov.uk/garden_home.asp The Pesticides Safety Directorate is part of the Department for Environment, Food and Rural Affairs. They provide a section for the home gardener that explains the risks of using pesticides, a database for checking out the chemicals you use and a list of banned chemicals.

Sustainable garden design

Sustainable gardens are about the sensitive use of the planet's resources to create beautiful spaces. This means being judicious in our use of water and hard landscaping (gravel, timber and concrete), and careful in our selection of plants – those that are well suited to the conditions that exist naturally in the garden are more likely to thrive without intervention. The following sites look at sustainability in garden design.

(There is more information in the section on water on page 84, which covers grey water retrieval systems.)

www.bethchatto.co.uk An inspirational gardener whose planting is both unusual and sustainable, planted as it is with drought-resistant plants. You can use the online catalogue to purchase plants.

www.cambridge-water.co.uk/about_you/save_garden.asp Good advice from this water company about saving water in your garden, paying attention to planting schemes and containers, and how to manage your lawn. There's a link to the University Botanic Garden in Cambridge, where a garden that doesn't need watering has been designed.

www.gardenvisit.com/garden_products/sustainable_design/sustai nable_gardens Has advice and articles on garden design. In addition, you can browse the site for inspiration, including sections on the Chelsea Flower Show.

www.permaculture.org.uk Permaculture is about creating sustainable human habitats by following nature's patterns.

www.rhs.org.uk/advice/watering.asp More advice about reducing the demand for watering with information on planting schemes and plants.

www.thedesignofgardens.com A site dedicated to sustainable landscape and garden design information set up by a landscape gardener. There are lists of tolerant plants, design and construction notes, and some really interesting articles under 'subject threads'. You can sign up to the newsletter and read the blog. The sales pitch for their services is low key, but you can arrange for a consultation too.

www.the-landscape-design-site.com This American landscape designer takes you through the principles of garden design. His section on xeriscaping is particularly relevant as it creates a water-wise garden, based on plants that are ideally suited to the conditions in the garden.

www.videojug.com/tag/garden-design Has introductions to a number of garden design topics, including wildlife gardens, ponds and recycled gardens.

Try these sites to find a designer:

http://gardendesign-uk.com

www.landscapeinstitute.org

Eden Project

In the 'horticulture' section at **www.edenproject.com** there is some very interesting information of interest to the environmentalist. Of course, it's not as interesting as being there.

Peat-free gardening

www.gloucestershirewildlifetrust.co.uk/index.php?section=environment:people:peatfree Sorry about the long URL, but this is a very good bullet-point style article from the Gloucester Wildlife Trust that encapsulates the issues and gives advice on using peat-free alternative composts.

www.thecompostshop.co.uk You can order online from this manufacturer of peat-free compost. There is a range of other related goods too, such as composters, mulches and wormeries.

Composting

www.gardenorganic.org.uk The section 'what we do' has extensive information on composting.

www.ipcc.ie It's in the interests of the Irish Peatland Conservation Council to provide good composting information.

www.recyclenow.com Has a good introductory guide to composting, some factsheets and some celebrity quotes on the subject.

www.urbancomposting.com Technical details on all the different composting approaches and the unexpectedly wide range of composting systems available.

Garden furniture and accessories

Many of the general garden sites mentioned previously have ranges of garden furniture. Please see the section on wood on page 71 for wood certification schemes before buying garden furniture.

www.arborvetum.co.uk Reclaimed teak furniture from Arbor Vetum with a good environmental ethos.

www.britisheco.com A small selection of furniture made by a charity that trains individuals with learning disabilities.

www.oakgardenfurniture.com Crafted garden furniture in oak.

www.henandhammock.co.uk Beautifully designed garden furniture, hammocks, lighting, play items and stuff for the potting shed, all made from sustainable materials.

www.rawstudio.co.uk Wonderful, wild and creative designs including hanging chairs and exdecks (wooden deckchairs). Their room system can also be made for use outdoors.

www.reelfurniture.co.uk Unusual and characterful garden furnishings made from recycled timber at David Meddings Design.

www.solarilluminations.co.uk A wide selection of solar-powered outdoor lighting.

www.thenaturalstore.co.uk Has a range of garden furniture, solar lights, garden toys and accessories.

Landscape materials

www.dunweedin.co.uk Rubber crumb for lawns and rubber chippings for landscaping borders or pathways, all made from recycled tyres.

www.ecomerchant.co.uk An ecologically sound builder's merchant with a good range of natural stone paving, sleepers, bricks and rainwater collection systems.

www.lankhorst.co.uk Recycled plastic is used to make decking and fencing.

www.railwaysleeper.com For railway sleepers and ideas on what to do with them.

Allotments

www.allotment.org.uk Forums, extensive information, links, diaries, recipes, photos and a shop.

www.allotments-uk.com Whether you want to find an allotment or learn more about it, the links are probably here, but the site is really hard to navigate.

www.nsalg.org.uk The united voice of the allotment movement. Join here, be represented and get their magazine, discounted insurance and seeds. Take advantage of their advice service, if you've still got questions to ask.

Miscellaneous

http://blueforest.com If you can afford more than £12,000 for a treehouse, this is the site for you.

www.gabrielash.com For the RHS range of greenhouses.

www.thewillowbank.com Will design and fit living willow features, or there are kits and instructions online. This is a lovely and natural way to design garden features such as arches, arbours and fencing.

Cut flowers

The reliance of African communities on cash crops such as flowers raises concern, particularly if land and water previously used for growing food is turned over to flower cultivation. There are worries too about the lack of regulation in the use of pesticides and herbicides, which threaten the environment as well as workers' health. Many of these workers are also children and paid a pittance. Air miles used in the transportation of flowers is a further disincentive to buying imported flowers.

The answer is to buy British-grown flowers, although the energy used to grow flowers in hothouses must also be taken into consideration. If you are uncertain as to the source of the flowers you are buying, look for the logo 'fair flowers fair plants'. For their policies see **www.fairflowersfairplants.com**.

If you want to say it with flowers, but feel uncomfortable with the choices, why not send the seeds instead? **www.flower-seed-gifts.co.uk** has some brilliant gift ideas that will last longer than a few days; **www.passiflora-uk.co.uk/gifts.shtml** offers just passion-flowers and **www.tree2mydoor.com** mainly trees.

www.cornishflowers.com Freshly picked, seasonal flowers from Cornwall delivered by first class mail.

www.davidaustinroses.com Beautiful English rose bouquets.

www.flowers.org.uk Promoting commercially cut flowers grown in the UK. The site has a really informative sections on cut flowers and plants ('flower facts and 'plant facts'). Select the species from a pull-down menu and up comes the history and care instructions.

www.johnlewis.com The flowers are imported but at least 25 per cent of them are Fairtrade.

www.scillyflowers.co.uk Flowers year round from a family farm in the Scilly Isles. They are not organic, but the flowers are sent by post.

www.tofc.co.uk Buy naturally grown seasonal flowers from a company that intends to be carbon neutral in 2008. They do source from 'far and wide' but are encouraging local growers to become organic.

www.valueflowers.net An ethically inspired online florist that uses organic, or in transition to organic, flower farms in England and the Channel Isles. Some of the flowers and plants that they sell are exotic, but all have been grown in the UK. They also sell gifts and chocolates.

www.wigglywigglers.co.uk Another source of seasonal English flowers.

Facts

- It is an offence under Section 1 of the Wildlife and Countryside Act of 1981 to intentionally take, damage or destroy the nest of any wild bird while it is in use or being built. So be careful when hedge trimming.

- More weedkiller is used per acre in the domestic garden than on the farm.

- Since 1945, 94 per cent of lowland raised peat bogs have vanished.

- A correctly made compost bin can reach 65 degrees Celcius.

- Three types of bacteria work in a compost heap: Psychrophiles at zero to 13 degrees Celcius, mesophiles at 15 to 40 degrees and thermophiles at 45 to 70 degrees.

- Hosepipes use up to 1,000 litres of water per hour.

- A garden hose left on for an hour can use as much water as four people use in a day.

- Only one in ten cut flowers bought in the UK are grown in the UK.

Living

Food

Shopping and the supermarkets

Around three-quarters of all food sales in Britain take place in the supermarket and the food we eat is responsible for almost one-third of the average family's impact on climate change. Clearly, there is huge potential here for the supermarkets to make it easier for the consumer to make positive choices.

The shift in public awareness and the demand for more sustainable produce has driven the supermarkets to make rapid changes in their policies. The following pages make for interesting reading; however, it will be interesting to see if these good intentions are followed up with good practice. The National Consumer Council is keeping a watching brief on this issue and found that no supermarkets were doing well across the board. Read the report at **www.ncc.org.uk** (follow the link to 'food' then 'spotlight on grocers').

See how your preferred supermarket intends to address the sustainability agenda:

http://plana.marksandspencer.com

www.asda-corporate.com

www.co-operative.co.uk/en/corporate/sustainability

www.morrisons.co.uk/Our-fresh-food

www.sainsburys.co.uk/aboutus/policies/policies.htm

www.tesco.com/greenerliving

www.waitrose.com/food/foodissuesandpolicies

Farmers' markets, farm shops and boxes

The received wisdom is to shop in small local shops and buy local produce wherever possible. As a consequence, buying direct from the producer is gaining in popular appeal. Both this section and the next cover organic and non-organic foods, but all are responsible suppliers. The following sites should help you track down local food in your area.

www.abelandcole.co.uk A well-established organic delivery scheme that allows you to add extra grocery items of your choice. They do not delivery nationwide but there is a locator.

www.boxscheme.org An organic produce directory.

www.farmersmarkets.net For details of the National Farmers' Retail and Markets Association (FARMA) certified farmers' markets that are genuinely offering local produce.

www.farmshopping.net Find a farm shop near you.

www.freerangereview.com A review and directory in a wide range of categories; particularly good for local box schemes.

www.localfoodweb.co.uk Helps to track down good food on your doorstep, from farm shops and speciality food retailers, to farmers' markets and village stores.

www.riverford.co.uk Another vegetable box scheme that covers most of southern and eastern England.

www.wen.org.uk/local_food/index.htm The excellent Women's Environmental Network (WEN) Local Food campaign and associated resources.

www.wewantrealfood.co.uk A directory of farmers' markets, farm shops and box schemes, with advice and information on seasonal foods and how to break the supermarket habit.

www.whyorganic.org A site sponsored by the Soil Association, which promotes organic farming in the UK. They provide a good directory of organic local suppliers, health advice, recipes and information on the 'big issues'.

Online and mail order grocery suppliers

There are an ever-increasing number of online suppliers. The following are directory sites that will help you find one that caters to your needs. You will find lists of specialist producers such as butchers and fishmongers below.

http://thefoody.com An online resource that has loads of information about British and Irish food and a database of mail order and online suppliers.

www.bigbarn.co.uk An online speciality food marketplace that aims to provide everyone in the country with a complete shopping basket of local foods in one delivery.

www.ethicalfoods.co.uk A wide range of foods, all ethically sound and available to order online.

www.goodnessdirect.co.uk A good ethical and environmental policy underlies this online supermarket, which sells around 4,000 lines. These include fresh and frozen foods and a good selection of ready meals.

www.organicdelivery.co.uk Has a wide range of goods, originally aimed at the London market but branching out countrywide.

www.swaddles.co.uk Organic grocers and butchers with a wide range of produce on offer, including ready meals and wines.

www.ukfoodonline.co.uk An independent online directory of suppliers of good-quality food and drink from UK producers. Buy online or by mail order.

www.upstart.coop/page36.html Information on how to set up your own wholefood co-op.

Slow food

The international Slow Food movement (**www.slowfood. org.uk**) was set up by Italians in response to the fast food chains' global spread. Basically, it is an association of foodies who meet together 'in convivium' to enjoy good, regional food and drink that is traditionally grown and lovingly cooked. Part of their mission is to protect biodiversity, promote sustainability and prevent the exploitation of producers.

Food miles

The transportation of food accounts for nearly 30 per cent of the heavy goods traffic on the roads. The green solution includes eating local foods and avoiding unseasonable imports, especially those that have been transported by air. Miles can also be avoided by buying locally in small shops, thereby cutting out the need to travel to out-of-town stores. When you do need the supermarket, sensible time management might enable you to stop as you pass it on your way elsewhere, so avoiding a special trip. Buying bulky groceries online or using the supermarket home delivery service is also good environmental practice – having a single vehicle making several deliveries in an area makes more sense than all of us trailing out to the supermarket in our cars.

There are some dilemmas though. For instance, imported Spanish tomatoes may have travelled to reach us but may still have a lower overall carbon footprint than British ones grown under artificial heat in a greenhouse. Then, should you buy imported organic beans from Kenya or non-organic ones grown nearer to home? These and other issues are addressed on the following sites.

www.carolinelucasmep.org.uk Green Party MEP Caroline Lucas has done some excellent work exposing the absurdity of European trade where countries simultaneously import and export the same produce in the name of competition and free trade. Read her reports 'Stopping the Great Food Swap' and 'Local Food: Benefits and Opportunities'.

www.new-agri.co.uk/07/02/pov.php A considered article from the *New Agriculturist*.

www.fwi.co.uk/gr/foodmiles *Farmer's Weekly* ran a campaign on food miles in 2006, but the information is still valid.

www.trulylocal.co.uk Has some practical tips.

Fairtrade and ethical concerns

Though not wholly concerned with the green agenda per se, workers' rights and respect for developing world communities are certainly of concern to anyone interested in sustainability.

www.actionaid.org.uk This charity is campaigning for new laws on corporate responsibility in the developing world, while the linked 'Target Poverty' drive enables individuals and businesses to get involved.

www.ethicaltrade.org Several of the major supermarkets are signed up to the Ethical Trading Initiative, which is working to ensure decent working conditions for the people who produce the goods they sell and to ensure a responsible supply chain.

www.fairtrade.org.uk The Fairtrade label appears on certified products and provides an independent guarantee that disadvantaged producers in the developing world are getting a fair deal. The site also provides information on how your workplace, café, school or town can join the scheme.

www.oxfam.org.uk/generationwhy/do_something/ethical Oxfam's excellent pages aimed at young people.

www.sustainweb.org The alliance for better food and farming advocates policies that enhance the welfare of people and animals, improve the working environment and promote equity through a variety of initiatives.

www.traidcraft.co.uk A Christian charity that combines a trading company and a development charity; they offer a range of goods for sale online.

www.ukfg.org.uk The UK Food Group is a network of non-governmental organisations that are concerned about global food and agricultural issues. There is some serious work going on within this organisation, which is reflected in the articles available to download.

Farming

There are numerous green issues to be explored around farming and the countryside. Balancing the demand for cheap food and a sustainable attitude towards biodiversity and the landscape is fraught with difficulties. Often this results in compromises that many are unwilling to condone. The following are websites on the subject.

http://forum.fwag.org/pubview.phtml?c1=7 Environmentally Responsible Farming has some excellent, simple guidance for farmers on good practice and biodiversity, which is assessable and of interest to the consumer.

www.animalaid.org.uk Campaigns for better animal welfare in order to lessen the suffering farmed animals endure; they aim to convince people not to eat meat.

www.cpre.org.uk The Campaign for the Protection of Rural England works to promote a sustainable future for the English countryside. There is information on their campaigns and how you can join the fight to defend it from detrimental development and promote positive farming practices; includes a local food initiative.

www.defra.gov.uk The official take on agriculture, rural affairs, fisheries and the environment. Their principles are sound, but action needs to be taken if their words are to be more than simply good intentions. The site says, 'The overarching challenge for Defra (Department for Environment, Food and Rural Affairs) is to enable everyone to live within our environmental means. This is most clearly exemplified by the need to tackle climate change internationally and through domestic action to reduce greenhouse gas emissions, and secure a healthy, resilient, productive and diverse natural environment.' A visit here is quite encouraging.

www.factoryfarming.org.uk A truly alarming site that would motivate anyone to avoid mass-produced poultry and meat.

www.leafuk.org LEAF (Linking Environment and Farming) is a body that promotes 'integrated farming' that can produce affordable food in harmony with the environment. The site provides information and ideas for good farm management and details of courses and workshops.

www.wholesome-food.org.uk The WFA symbol is used by producers who grow and process their produce using sustainable and non-polluting methods.

www.whyfarmingmatters.co.uk Aims to champion British farming and communicate what farmers are doing for diversity, climate change, food standards and the economy.

The organic movement
www.ifoam.org The International Federation of Organic Agriculture Movements (IFOAM) unites 750 member organisations in 108 countries. The four principles of organic cultivation are laid out: the principles of health, ecology, fairness and care. They supply loads of information about the movement and its projects.

www.linksorganic.com An international directory of links in a wide range of categories from agricultural supplies to co-operatives to marketing.

www.organicfarmers.uk.com An organic assurance certification scheme.

www.planorganic.com News, articles and loads of links on matters organic, including lists of suppliers in Ireland and the UK.

www.soilassociation.org The Soil Association symbol is found on around 70 per cent of British organic produce.

Sustainweb's seven principles of sustainable food

1. Use local, seasonally available ingredients.

2. Buy organic or food farmed with respect to the environment.

3. Limit the consumption of foods of animal origin.

4. Exclude fish species identified as most 'at risk' by the Marine Conservation Society, and choose fish only from sustainable sources.

5 Choose Fairtrade-certified products.

6. Avoid bottled water.

7. Promote health and wellbeing by cooking with generous portions of vegetables, fruit and starchy staples; cut down on salt, fats and oils; cut out artificial additives.

www.sustainweb.org

Meat and dairy farming

www.britegg.co.uk The British Egg Information Service accounts for the six million eggs produced in the UK. Enter the code on your egg and locate the farm it comes from.

www.ciwf.org.uk Lobbies to improve standards of animal husbandry and to end cruel factory-farming practices.

www.ndfas.org.uk Setting the standards for the dairy industry.

www.rspca.org.uk The freedom food logo is the RSPCA's farm-assurance labelling scheme that guarantees that farms have been inspected and meet minimum requirements.

www.yeovalleyorganic.co.uk This successful organic dairy producer shows how organic, sustainable production can also be a commercial enterprise.

Online meat retailers
http://highlandgame.com Sells fresh venison and partridge plus has recipes and information.

www.blackface.co.uk Seasonal, regional and traceable; this Scottish site supplies boxes of lamb, mutton, beef, pork and a good selection of game and haggis.

www.donaldrussell.co.uk An award-winning butcher that offers a wide range of other produce as well as meats. It also offers a reduced packaging option.

www.helenbrowningorganics.co.uk Buying advice, recipes and an online shop from this Wiltshire organic farmer. Includes a good veal guide.

www.realmeat.co.uk For information about the farming philosophy of this Wiltshire company and details about their shops and online service.

www.richardwoodall.com If you can't live without Cumberland sausages, then get them here; you'll find plenty of cured meats too.

www.sausagelinks.co.uk All about sausages and there's a search facility so you can track down a reputable sausage shop near you.

www.traditionalbutcher.co.uk Based in Herefordshire and knows a thing or two about meat. You can buy meats and deli products online.

www.trealyfarm.com An online charcuterie for cured meats.

Farming issues

Pesticides and residues
www.pan-uk.org Pesticide Action Network works to eliminate the dangers of toxic pesticides in both the UK and overseas. In addi-

tion to their work with the agricultural community, they provide information on gardening and dealing with domestic pests. There is also a link to the comprehensive US database on pesticides at **www.pesticideinfo.org**.

www.pesticide-residue.co.uk Even using pesticides within the guidelines may result in a crop with a detectable pesticide level. This residue-testing company has some interesting information on pesticides and their associated risks.

www.pesticides.gov.uk The government's pages on the workings of the Pesticide Residues Committee.

GM food
http://genewatch.org A non-profit organisation that monitors the advance in genetic technology.

www.food.gov.uk/gmfoods From the government's point of view.

www.greenpeace.org.uk/gm The case against GM foods.

www.monsanto.co.uk Monsanto is one of the biggest companies promoting GM foods. See the issues from their point of view.

www.mutatoes.org A group campaigning against GM.

www.sirc.org/gate/gm_food.html A comprehensive reading list from the Social Issues Research Centre.

www.ucsusa.org The Union of Concerned Scientists has an exposé on food, including the GM debate.

Irradiation
http://en.wikipedia.org/wiki/Food_irradiation Quite a detailed, impartial section on irradiation technologies and safety from the online encyclopaedia.

www.foodcomm.org.uk/irradiation_probs.htm A good overview of the issues followed by a set of links.

Allergies and food intolerances
www.earthways.co.uk/enumbers.html Three lists of E numbers: red

for the most dangerous; amber for those that raise some concern; green for those considered safe.

www.foodsmatter.com A substantial archive of articles and research material on allergy and intolerance and related conditions.

Food labelling schemes
www.eatwell.gov.uk/foodlabels The low-down on the various labelling schemes.

www.myredtractor.co.uk A farm standard-assurance scheme. Criticisms of this scheme can be found on the Friends of the Earth and RSPCA websites (**www.foe.co.uk** and **www.rspca.org.uk**).

Fish and fishing
We are told that eating fish a couple of times a week is good for our health, but at what cost to the marine environment, when fish stocks are rapidly depleting as the drag nets scoop out everything in their path? Fish farms would seem to be the answer, but it turns out that many of these are disastrous for local biodiversity and are a source of marine pollution.

The most detailed site on this topic is **www.mcsuk.org** by the Marine Conservation Society, whose remit is to campaign for clean seas and beaches, sustainable fisheries and protection for all marine life. The related site **www.fishonline.org** is the consumer site aimed at helping people eat the right fish from a conservation point of view. They provide lots of background information on fish, fish farming and fishing methods. The good purchasing guide and the section on fish to avoid are both really useful.

www.environmentaldefense.org Their section on oceans covers responsible fishing and has an eco-friendly seafood selector, which, although aimed at an American market, is mostly relevant. The section on health has interesting information on contaminants found in fish, such as mercury, pesticides and industrial chemicals.

www.friendofthesea.org Buying their labelled fish ensures that the fisheries target stocks that are not overexploited, and use fishing methods that don't impact on the seabed and that generate less than average (8 per cent) discards. Browse under 'sustainable seafood marketplace' for suppliers.

www.seafish.org Promotes good-quality, sustainable fish and links to their Responsible Fishing Scheme website, with its own labelling scheme that aims to encourage fishermen to sign up to their code of practice.

www.wwf.org.uk The Worldwide Fund for Nature also works to stop over-fishing and protect marine habitats.

Online fishmongers
www.andyrace.co.uk Peat-smoked salmon is a speciality and all the fish sold is caught by local boats to ensure quality. It is seafish endorsed and there are some organic products too.

www.graigfarm.co.uk/shop.php For their sustainably farmed fish including organic salmon and cod, pot-caught crab and smoked wild fish.

www.nocatch.co.uk An animated, talking website from a supplier of sustainable fish products, including fishfingers, to major retailers. There is a locator to find your nearest supplier.

www.fishinabox.co.uk An online supplier that has signed up to the 'Tracefish' project (see earlier details on the Marine Conservation Society).

Vegetarian and vegan options

Without a doubt, a vegetarian lifestyle helps reduce your environmental impact. With affluence comes a rise in meat consumption, which is estimated to double by 2050. Add to this an increasing global population and the need to produce livestock intensively becomes compelling. Intensive agriculture brings deforestation and soil erosion, makes vast demands on water supplies and produces huge qualities of greenhouse gas emissions. A vegetarian diet makes only one-third of the demand on global resources as a meat-based diet; a vegan diet, based only on plant food, impacts considerably less than this.

www.beyondveg.com Articles on a number of alternative diets.

www.fruitarian.com Cutting the diet down to fruit only and how to do it.

www.living-foods.com Devoted to the subject of eating only raw foods.

www.vegansociety.com The Vegan Society provides lots of environmental reasons why veganism is a good environmental option. The site has supporting information and links to other related sites and books.

www.veganstore.co.uk Offers over 800 products suitable for vegans.

www.vegsoc.org The Vegetarian Society promotes a meat-free diet as the green option. The site contains advice and help on becoming a vegetarian, a business section and recipes. It also features the Cordon Vert cookery school and there's a good education section for teachers and young people.

Celebrity chefs

www.jamieoliver.com Jamie Oliver and his hobbyhorses.

www.rickstein.com Check out his 'food heros' for excellent suppliers of British produce.

www.rivercottage.net Hugh Fearnley-Whittingstall and his individual quest for good food.

General food-related sites

www.eatwell.gov.uk A guide to healthy eating including a Body Mass Index (BMI) calculator, information about dietary requirements for life's different stages and a guide to the quagmire that is labelling.

www.foodcomm.org.uk A brilliant campaigning organisation that keeps a watchful eye over the food we eat, which, they claim, should be tasty, nutritious and safe. They also investigate the hidden costs of mass marketing and food production. Subscribe to their informative magazine on this site or browse through for some fascinating yet scary insights.

www.foodstandards.gov.uk An excellent attempt to keep the public informed about food-related issues, with easily accessible, high-quality information covering nutrition, GM issues, safety and hygiene, and up-to-date news items.

www.lovefoodhatewaste.com Cutting down on waste is common sense – it saves both the environment and money. This website is full of ideas on how to shop sensibly and store food safely.

www.raisingkids.co.uk/food/food.asp From breastfeeding to teenage diets, there's quality coverage here.

www.sustainweb.org Sustain is an alliance of national organisations that advocates improved food and agriculture policies. There are some high-quality documents available to download and project information. The one on sustainable food is particularly relevant.

www.thewi.org.uk The Women's Institute has a noble reputation for good food. They have a number of campaigns regarding food, waste, climate change and sustainable consumption.

www.tradingstandards.gov.uk For protection against the rogues.

www.ucsusa.org/food_and_environment The American Union of Concerned Scientists scrutinises food and farming technology and lobbies on issues such as antibiotic overuse, GM foods and American food subsidies, and their effects on production.

Bad food Britain

This *Observer* article by Joanna Blythman at **http://observer. guardian.co.uk/foodmonthly/futureoffood/story/0,,1970541,00 .html** considers what food in Britain might be like in the year 2050 if we continue with contemporary trends – an interesting but bleak read.

Drink

Organic and Fairtrade tea and coffee have gained ground in recent years, and the big tea and coffee companies are beginning to change their ways in the face of public concern. Single companies such as Green and Black in the world of chocolate and Clipper teas do a great job of raising awareness that there is a choice to be made. Organic beers and wines are becoming more widely available at the supermarket, but only small inroads have been made into the vast alcohol market.

Tea and coffee
www.cafedirect.co.uk Bringing Fairtrade coffee into the mainstream.

www.clipper-teas.com Probably the best-known organic tea and coffee company in the high street.

www.ethicalteapartnership.org Sixty brands have signed up to this initiative, including most of the big players. Their ultimate goal is to ensure that 100 per cent of the tea bought by members is produced in a socially responsible way.

www.fairtrade.org.uk For a list of Fairtrade-certified tea and coffee brands.

www.ico.org The International Coffee Organization is an inter-governmental agency set up by the UN to promote coffee trade and deal with associated issues, including sustainable production and improved living standards for those working in the industry.

Alcohol

Here the issues are around the chemicals used in the processing of drinks and the herbicide and pesticide use during the farming process. There is the ever present fact of food miles too. For instance, beers brewed abroad (as well as those brewed in the UK) tend to be made from imported hops and other ingredients. Adding this to the mileage cost of travel to your local, and an imported lager could clock up over 24,000 beer miles.

Several companies offer organic wines, beers, ciders and spirits online. You can also buy vegan wines: those that do not use gelatine, albumin or other fish-derived agents in the clarification process. Here are a few to choose from:

www.festivalwines.co.uk

www.vintageroots.co.uk

www.vinceremos.co.uk

www.vineorganic.co.uk

Chocolate

Some of the supermarkets, including Co-op, Tesco, Marks and Spencer and Waitrose, are now selling Fairtrade chocolate, some of which is also organic. Oxfam sell a selection in their shops too.

www.chocs.co.uk The Hotel Chocolat Tasting Club is a haven for chocoholics and has a good ethical policy.

www.greenandblacks.com Probably the best-known organic chocolate on the high street, but you can shop online too.

Facts

- **More than one in five British adults is obese.**

- **Food and drink companies spent £700 million on advertising in the UK (2006).**

- **To claim that a product is 'reduced fat', the amount of fat must** be at least 25 per cent lower than the standard product.

- Ninety-five per cent of the fruit and 50 per cent of the vegetables we eat are imported.

- A basket of 26 imported organic foods may have travelled the equivalent of six times around the equator.

- In New Zealand 43 per cent of greenhouse gases generated come from flatulent sheep, while in France 15 per cent of methane is emitted by cows.

- More than 750 million broiler chickens (chickens bred for their meat) are reared and slaughtered each year in the UK; 98 per cent are reared in intensive indoor systems and less than 2 per cent are free-range or organic.

- In the last 30 years, 50 per cent of British pear orchards and over 60 per cent of apple orchards have been destroyed.

- During the last century, Europe lost 75 per cent of its food product diversity: 30,000 vegetable varieties disappeared.

- One-third of food bought in the UK ends up being thrown away.

Shopping

There are an impressive number of eco-lifestyle online stores to choose from. They tend to all stock a basic range of products covering home and personal care, eco gadgets and gifts, while some also stock food and clothing. They are all different and, as you explore them, you will find some more to your taste than others.

Eco comparison sites

Before you shop, there are a number of sites that help you make good green choices – particularly useful if you are making a purchase such as a washing machine or mobile phone.

www.ethicalconsumer.org Check out products before you buy at

Ethical Consumer magazine, where they expose the ethical information behind the big brand names. The site includes products to boycott, buyers' guides and ethical ratings.

www.ethiscore.org A non-profit organisation that enables the consumer to identify the best products to buy and the companies to avoid by calculating an 'ethical score' out of 20. They look at goods in over 160 product areas. You have to subscribe to gain access to the entire site.

www.gooshing.co.uk If you want to find the most ethical lawnmower or discover which mobile phone company has the best ethical policies, this site is another source of such information. They compare goods in a wide range of categories and have researched each manufacturer's background; for instance, whether or not they make political donations. There is also an ethical marketplace that promotes the goods and services that they endorse.

www.hippyshopper.com A lively site that is an asset to anyone interested in ethical culture. It provides daily advice, product news and all the information that you need to make you go green.

www.ibuygreen.co.uk A shopping comparison site that helps you find the best internet deals on the best energy-rated appliances and household goods, including mobile phones, personal audio and kitchen appliances.

General stores

If you can't find what you want in the sites below, check out a directory site such as **www.thegreenshoppingguide.co.uk**.

http://alotofshopping.co.uk A guilt-free ethical shopping site for all things organic and eco. They have a good selection, including some food, gifts, beauty and household products.

http://ecotopia.co.uk This site was set up with assistance from The Prince's Trust with the aim of helping people adopt lower impact lifestyles. The range is good, while the bulk buying section is an unusual feature that makes good sense.

www.allthingsgreen.net This site has a good choice of eco-friendly products from small, UK-based companies. There are sections on home and garden, clothing and fashion, health and beauty, baby and toddler, food and drink, stationery and cards.

www.ecohamster.co.uk Offers eco alternatives to many ordinary products such as eco chargers, henna hair dye and totally degradable plastic bags.

www.ecoutlet.co.uk A good assortment of domestic products and gifts are on sale here. We particularly liked the wine glasses made from cut-down wine bottles. You can collect eco points while you shop and when you've got sufficient they will send a donation to a designated charity of your choice.

www.ecozone.co.uk Environmentally friendly household products and eco gadgets.

www.ethicalonestopshop.com With thousands of eco friendly, Fairtrade, natural, vegan and recycled products in all the usual categories, this is one of the best online shops around.

www.fairtrade.org.uk Home of the Fairtrade Foundation, which exists to enable poor craftsman and workers to get a better deal. They have a list of products and the site directs you to an online retailer.

www.getethical.com This site has a wide variety of ethically produced and sourced products plus advice, links, a blog and a newsletter. Their selection includes technology, flowers, clothing, sports goods and items for the home.

www.greenandeasy.co.uk They provide a range of products and services for people who are looking to be more environmentally friendly in their everyday lives – everything from washing-up liquid to wind-up lanterns and tents.

www.greenshop.co.uk Encourages customers to live lightly on the planet by providing hundreds of sustainable and low-impact products for the home, including paint and household cleaners.

www.naturalcollection.com A comprehensive range of products that includes clothing, food and cosmetics. There are also garden and outdoor living goods, and office supplies.

www.nigelsecostore.com Nigel is inspired by eco products and ideas that solve environmental challenges. He sources products that use recycled materials, don't pollute, are natural or organic, are functional and look great.

www.traidcraftshop.co.uk A selection of crafts, foods and other goods from around the world.

Shopper's blog

See **http://ecofabulous.blogs.com** for one American's view of the world of eco consumerism. She offers to be your dedicated guide to 'finding and sharing sexy, sustainable products and services'.

Gift shops

www.afrigoods.org A nice selection of African curios, sculptures and a range of other artefacts, including bags, sculpture, leather goods and jewellery.

www.btgiftsandaccessories.co.uk Lovely arts and crafts sourced from small co-operatives throughout the world. Includes such items as photo albums, textiles, jewellery and candles.

www.cardaid.co.uk Charity Christmas cards.

www.goodgifts.org Online, charitable, alternative gift catalogue for all occasions. You could find yourself giving a row of native English hedgerow or sponsoring eye tests in India.

www.greatgifts.org World Vision's charity website offers an alternative, online gift catalogue.

www.onevillage.org Specialising in ethnic Fairtrade products, mainly for the home.

www.tree2mydoor.com Send a tree or a wildflower seed package as a gift in place of cut flowers. There are also suggested packages for wedding gifts, memorials and new baby gifts, amongst others.

Buy recycled and be guilt free

At **www.recycledproducts.org.uk** it's quite enlightening to see the range of products that can be made from recycled materials.

Bookshops

Don't forget that maybe the greenest option of all is to use the library service.

Environmental specialists

http://greenbooks.co.uk An independent publisher producing books on environmental and cultural issues. Download their catalogue to see their titles.

www.booksand.info For technical publications on the environment; not for the casual environmentalist.

www.earthscan.co.uk Books on sustainable development and environmental technology aimed at the professional end of the market.

www.eco-logicbooks.com A well-stocked bookshop that has recently also started to publish its own titles. They have a useful 'bookfinder' search facility and you can subscribe to the newsletter to keep abreast of new books.

www.green-shopping.co.uk Look under 'books' for a good range of titles well organised under a number of subheadings. They also sell *Permaculture Activist* magazine.

www.nhbs.com The Environmental Bookstore is full of books on wildlife, science and conservation. The site is well categorised and DVDs and some wildlife equipment are available too.

Recycled books

www.abebooks.co.uk A second-hand and rare book search that finds your title from the 110 million registered by 13,500 independent book dealers at this site. The books don't have to be anything special; used copies of last month's bestsellers are here too. The site also searches for new books.

www.greenmetropolis.com A great recycling initiative. Sell your old books and buy new ones with the credits at this fabulous online store. There is a small difference in cost between the two, but this covers the free postage and a small percentage goes to the Woodland Trust. You will be impressed by the range of titles on offer.

Release books

Go to **www.bookcrossing.com**, register the book on the site and mark it as part of the scheme, then leave the book in a café, on a train or anywhere else you fancy. You can sit back and track the book's fate as other readers' hand it on.

Facts

- Twenty-seven per cent of greenhouse gases comes from domestic energy use.

- Around a billion people worldwide have entered the twenty-first century unable to read a book.

- Almost £1 billion is spent on toys in the two weeks before Christmas.

- The Christmas luxury goods market is worth £35 billion.

- **A recent report from the Co-operative Bank showed that only 3 per cent of the UK market is devoted to green products.**

- **A poll in the Guardian showed that two-thirds of the British public would buy ethically if the opportunity presented itself.**

- **A plastic bag tax in Ireland has dramatically reduced the demand for new plastic bags, plus seen a 90 per cent drop in the number discarded.**

- **If everyone in the world lived as we do in the UK, we would need the resources of three planets to sustain us.**

Body products and health

Beauty and the chemical beast

It is true that the cosmetic industry is subject to numerous regulations that ensure products are safe for human use. It is also true to say that some chemicals that are perfectly safe when used alone may be less benign when used as part of a chemical cocktail.

One report from the US National Institute of Occupational Safety and Health found that 884 chemicals used in personal care products and cosmetics are known to be toxic to some degree. The issue is of concern because the skin easily absorbs some of these chemicals, which then find their way into the cells in our bodies. The precise number of chemicals found, for instance, in breast milk or tumours may be contentious, and how many of these originated in beauty products is speculative; however, the fact that they have been found is not. The converse is true. Some highly advertised products extol the virtue of ingredients with impressive chemical names, hoping that the consumer will be impressed by the science; however, many – such as collagen, elastin and similar proteins – are made up of molecules too large to enter the epidermis, so they cannot be absorbed.

Below are some sites that will help you do the research to see if you are being taken in by the hype. They inform you which chemicals raise the most concerns. There are also a number of organic suppliers listed.

www.cosmeticdatabase.com Ignore the request to give your details and enter the site. You'll find a search facility that allows you to type in the products you use and back will come information regarding the chemicals you are exposing yourself to, the risks you are taking and whether or not the manufacturer tests on animals. It is American, so some products may not be listed, but 25,000 are. Salutary reading.

www.hallgold.com/toxic-chemical-ingredients-directory.htm For a complete list of chemicals, their function and their possible toxicity.

www.theallergysite.co.uk/cosmetics.html A shorter list primarily aimed at allergy sufferers.

www.wen.org.uk/cosmetics/resources.htm The Woman's Environmental Network has produced an excellent briefing entitled 'Getting Lippy: Cosmetics, Toiletries and the Environment'. It's available as a PDF file and it discusses the perils of the cosmetic industry, including an exposé of the science and the concerns raised by some of the chemicals commonly in use. The site also covers issues such as animal testing, GM and kinder alternatives. There are a number of associated factsheets under 'resources' which are shorter, informative and well designed.

Organic and ethical suppliers

www.greenpeople.co.uk Awarded 'best organic range' in the 2008 Natural Health Beauty Awards, Green People have a comprehensive product range that includes a few cosmetics, babies' and children's products, sun cream and travel-size goods too.

www.honestycosmetics.co.uk A reputable company with impeccable credentials. They sell their own products, plus those from complementary manufacturers whose products are compatible with their own standards.

www.nealsyardremedies.com One of the most established organic body care shops, which sells a comprehensive range of own-brand products as well as herbal, flower and homeopathic remedies. They sell base products too, so you can blend your own.

www.thebodyshopinternational.com The Body Shop has always maintained that a business can be both profitable and responsible. They have sound ethical and environmental principles and there is a lot about them on the site. The products are of a good quality too, and are now available online.

Shop online

We all have our own personal favourites, so here is quite a long list of companies that make organic products. Generally, the ranges are not huge, so browse these sites to find the products that appeal to you.

www.akamuti.co.uk

www.beingorganic.com

www.essential-care.co.uk

www.faithinnature.co.uk

www.motherearth.co.uk

www.primavera.co.uk

www.renskincare.com

www.simplysoaps.com

www.skincarecafe.com

www.spieziaorganics.com

www.weleda.co.uk

Extreme cosmetics

For a look at botox, collagen injections, peels and other invasive therapies, the BBC has an excellent section examining the pros and cons with video clips and animation (**www.bbc. co.uk/science/hottopics/extremecosmetics**).

Natural hair dye

Commercial hair dyes contain a powerful mixture of chemicals, some of which are potentially carcinogenic. Some cause cancer in rats and others are known to be dangerous if ingested, although the jury is out as to whether they are toxic when absorbed through the skin. Amongst these are PPDs (phenylenediamines), which are used in all permanent dyes because they are the only colour pigments that will fix dye to the hair shaft. Ammonia is used in most dyes as a bleaching agent. This damages the outer layer of the hair and repeated applications permanently affect hair strength and texture.

Natural dyes are less chemically dependant, although the only truly natural dye is henna. However, in 2002 the European Union's scientific committee on cosmetic products found that the chemical lawsone, found in henna, is toxic to kidneys, the blood supply and parts of the stomach if used in high concentrations. The only really safe option, it appears, is to grow old gracefully!

Henna

www.henna-boy.co.uk For henna hair and body dye. They offer a fresh pre-mix service. Hidden at the bottom of the page under 'recipes' is good up-to-date information on using henna.

www.lush.co.uk/categories/Henna_44.aspx For solid henna dyes and how to use them.

www.worldsend.co.uk/henna-hair-dye-60-c.asp Suppliers of liquid henna dyes ranging from black, brown, blonde and red.

Natural dyes

www.danielfieldmailorder.co.uk The Watercolours range claims to 100 per cent cover grey hair without the use of ammonia. It varies from permanent to semi-permanent (six washes) depending on whether it is applied to wet, damp or dry hair.

www.gentlebodycare.co.uk and **www.goodnessdirect.co.uk** Both sell Herbatint, a permanent dye with a good colour range. They are formulated using low levels of pharmaceutical ingredients (including PPDs) and vegetal extracts; they do not contain ammonia. Vegetal is the semi-permanent sister product that contains no ammonia or PPDs.

www.naturesdream.co.uk Supplies Naturtint, a similar product to Herbatint.

www.suvarna.co.uk/hair-dyes.html Semi-permanent, 100 per cent natural, organic dyes made from henna and other natural products such as walnut shells and buckthorn.

Make sage and rosemary hair dye

Get the recipe at **www.pioneerthinking.com/graydye.html**. With repeated use it is claimed that this can cover grey hair.

Cruelty-free cosmetics

Seventy-nine per cent of us say that we would change to a brand that was not tested on animals given the information. That information is provided at **www.gocrueltyfree.org/companies.php**, which lists companies approved by the Humane Cosmetics Standard (HCS) or the Humane Household Products Standard (HHPS). **www.uncaged.co.uk/crueltyfree.htm** has a shorter good and bad company list. The Uncaged site also has good information on the law, science, animal rights and pet foods.

There is a problem with some products purporting to be 'not

tested on animals', which may be true for the shampoo or cream in question but may not be true for the ingredients that make up the product. It is good practice to choose products certified by a recognised agency.

Sanitary protection

An essential fact of life for half the world's population, but with each of us using 12,000 pads or tampons in a lifetime, sensible environmental considerations should be made.

www.grownupgreen.org.uk/library/?id=519 Has a good synopsis of the WEN briefing on the subject (**www.wen.org**).

www.mooncup.co.uk The reusable menstrual cup; those that have got used to it seem very happy, but check out independent user's reviews at **www.ciao.co.uk/Mooncup__5346101**.

www.treehuggermums.co.uk/articles/parenting/article.php?article= 100 and **www.femininezone.com/articles.php?a=readandaid=219** Both have considered articles on more environmentally friendly solutions.

Natural health

There is a resurgence of interest in natural health products, and alternative and complementary therapies. We are not qualified to comment on the efficacy of these, and would recommend that if you are unwell you seek the help of your doctor. However, these sites may be of interest.

http://nccam.nih.gov Home of the US National Centre for Complementary and Alternative Medicine, it's a good place for researching into any medicine before you take it.

www.alternativemedicines.co.uk Use the ailment search to find the right alternative products.

www.altmedicine.com You have to sign their disclaimer to gain access to material on the latest therapies and trends with articles and features. The site is supplemented by an excellent medical search engine, an overview of the major philosophies and associated healing techniques, plus a good set of related links.

www.eoco.org.uk The Essential Oil Company for aromatherapy.

www.herbs.org Look under 'resources' for a botanical gallery of medicinal plants and under 'greenpapers' for information about the herbs themselves. They can also help you find a practitioner.

www.homeopathyhome.com Slightly confusing to use but comprehensive.

www.homeopathy-soh.org Home of the Society of Homeopaths. They will help you find one that they have accredited and give you some background reading.

www.interconnections.co.uk A confusing portal but there is information on a wide range of therapies, including colour therapy, NLP, past-life counselling and holistic career counselling.

www.internethealthlibrary.com A good directory for alternative health sites. The A–Z of ailments is particularly useful and the section on environmental health issues links with Friends of the Earth and is interesting related reading.

www.medical-acupuncture.co.uk A good-looking site with information from the British Medical Acupuncture Society on the nature of acupuncture and where to find a practitioner in your area. There are also good links and information on courses. See also **www.acupuncture.org.uk** and **http://accupuncture.com**.

www.nimh.org.uk Find a qualified herbalist near you. If you are interested in training to be a herbalist, then there are links to courses.

www.therapy-world.co.uk A magazine-style site covering many different types of therapies with a good overview of all of them and some interesting articles.

www.thinknatural.com Has a mass of information on every aspect of natural health, including a comprehensive shop with loads of special offers and a very wide range of products.

Yoga

www.abc-of-yoga.com The background information on this site is excellent, with information on the history, yogic styles, mediation and the health benefits of yoga. The best bit is the comprehensive list of exercises (asanas) with clear photographs or illustrations to back up the instructions.

www.yogauk.com The yoga village provides information on the yoga scene in the UK. You can subscribe to their magazine or browse the links section, which has a comprehensive list of stores.

Facts

- **Up to 50 per cent of the cost of a perfume may be eaten up by the packaging and advertising.**

- **Eighty-nine per cent of 10,500 ingredients used in personal care have not been evaluated for human safety.**

- **Over three million animals are used for experiments in the UK every year.**

- **Over 7,000 different ingredients are available for use in the cosmetic industry, 1,000 of which function as either perfumes or aromatics.**

- **There is no legal definition of the word 'natural'; in fact, products only have to contain 1 per cent 'natural' ingredients to be labelled as natural.**

- **More than four million tampons and sanitary pads are flushed in the UK daily.**

Fashion and accessories

The media is full of fashion icons and many of us fall prey to its seduction. The green approach is to reduce the amount of clothes that you buy in the first place and to select natural fabrics, especially hemp or organically produced cotton or wool. Recycling clothing in both directions makes sense: sell or give away clothing that you do not need and buy from a charity shop or a site such as eBay. If you are going somewhere fancy, beg, borrow or hire.

www.pan-uk.org/Projects/Cotton argues the case for organic cotton, which they refer to as the 'moral fibre'. There is a salutary video on the site about the damaging health effects of pesticide use on human health in developing countries, and a useful consumer guide, which links to companies that use organic cotton in our county.

Fairtrade

Fairtrade is a big issue in the textile industry. We are all aware of the sweatshop regimes that are the backbone of the buy-cheap, buy-often clothing that we see on the high street. If you want to learn more about the consequences of that attitude on workers in the developing world visit **http://fashioninganethicalindustry.org**. They provide a selection of factsheets, information on how to source ethical raw materials, videos, teaching resources and links, should you wish to explore the topic further. You might feel motivated to join **www.cleanclothes.org**, a campaigning group focused on improving working conditions for textiles workers worldwide.

Keep it clean

When selecting clothing it is good practice to take note of the care instructions. Avoid dry cleaning like the plague, and try not to buy clothes that need ironing – not only does this save energy, but it saves time too. See page 79 for information on laundry and GreenEarth dry cleaning.

The high street

www.hm.com This shop is increasing its organic cotton range in 2008 due to its popularity.

www.marksandspencer.com They have a 'Greener Living' shop that has a good range of their hallmark clothing, home goods and gifts made from a range of Fairtrade, recycled and/or organic materials. There is also an ethical savings fund. At the time of writing, there wasn't a direct link on their homepage, so type 'greener living' into their site search engine to get you to there.

www.newlook.co.uk/women/organics/CollectionList.aspx For their range of dresses, tops and jeans made from organic cotton.

www.topshop.com A small, Fairtrade range. Unfortunately, the much-hyped collaboration with People Tree (**www.peopletree.co.uk**) was for a limited duration.

Online fashion

www.amoosi.co.uk Wonderful designer clothes made from classy, recycled fabrics.

www.clothworks.co.uk High-end, stylish women's wear in silks, natural cottons and hemp. Beautiful designs.

www.eco-boudoir.com Luxury lingerie with a clearish conscience.

www.greenfibres.com A Soil Association licensed company with a selection of men's, women's and children's wear. Their range covers not only towels and bed linen, but duvets, mattresses and beds as well. For more on children's clothing see page 138.

www.naturalcollection.com A good range of clothing for all the family including some footwear.

www.peopletree.co.uk Pioneers in Fairtrade, organic fashion with an excellent adult range. There are limited options for children and cotton jersey bed linen.

www.thenaturalstore.co.uk Has a good selection of lady's clothing including special occasion and everyday wear, lingerie and some shoes. There is also menswear, baby's and toddler's clothing and footwear.

Hemp

Hemp is an extraordinary material; it can be used for food, fuel and fibre and grows quickly without the need for pesticides. For information go to **www.houseofhemp.co.uk/hemp.html**.

Casuals and T-shirts

www.ascensionclothing.co.uk T-shirts, jeans and casual trousers for men and women made from organic cotton by a company with great eco credentials.

www.braintreehemp.co.uk An Australian company selling casual clothes made from hemp.

www.colonelkilgoreclothing.com For boarder's T-shirts.

www.dotrunshop.co.uk Only a few T-shirts; however; it's well worth visiting this unique site.

www.equop.com The site has a great selection of young designs, including hoodies.

www.fairtrademedia.co.uk Has plains and a few Fairtrade-themed T-shirts.

www.howies.co.uk Stylish casuals, some made from recycled cotton and organic cord.

www.patagonia.com For outdoor gear from a company with strong environmental credentials. Some of the clothing, including the fleece jackets and some of the footwear, are made from substantial quantities of recycled materials.

www.thehempstore.co.uk For a range of clothing and accessories made from hemp. There is also information on the site about hemp and why it is a good product for the eco-conscious consumer to buy.

www.thtc.co.uk Urban eco-wear.

www.tonictshirts.com A young man's range of printed and embroidered T-shirts with a humorous edge; also a few for women and children.

www.tshirtstudio.com Perfect if you wish to design your own T-shirt.

Shoes

There is a surprising range of shoes on offer that will lighten your environmental footprint. Some are stunning designer offers, others more rugged, and most are suitable for vegans.

www.beyondskin.co.uk A colourful and attractive range of vegan designer shoes for women.

www.earthandwear.com A range of casual canvas low-tops, high-tops, boots and sandals, including some made from hemp. Also jewellery, bags and purses.

www.ethicalwares.com Vegan, Fairtrade shoes for both men and women, including casual, street and smart shoes.

www.fairdealtrading.com Fair Deal Trading Partnership for footballs and trainers.

www.freerangers.co.uk Vegan-approved footwear, handmade in the UK.

www.hettyrose.co.uk Stunning, handmade, bespoke shoes made from vintage materials. They are expensive, but exquisite.

www.noharm.co.uk Cruelty-free, vegan, Italian-made footwear for men.

www.terraplana.com Has a sound ethical policy and uses chrome-free, vegetable-tanned leathers, recycled materials and E-leather.

The footwear ranges from the stylish and elegant to the flat and comfortable, for both men and women. Their range of 'worn again' recycled trainers are excellent.

Customise old clothes for a new life

Take a look at **www.bbc.co.uk/dna/h2g2/A20074899**.

Second-hand clothes

Here are some alternatives to eBay (**www.ebay.co.uk**).

www.maternityexchange.co.uk Buy or hire your maternity clothes.

www.touchlocal.com/nat/c-1755-Second+Hand+Designer+Clothes +Shops For a list of second-hand designer clothing shops nation-wide.

www.whatsmineisyours.com An internet swap shop for your unwanted clothes.

Why its hip to wear recycled

Check out **www.ethicsgirls.co.uk/recycledfashion**.

Make your own

www.drapersorganiccotton.co.uk Sells hemp by the metre.

www.greenfibres.com Has a small range of yarns and fabrics by the metre.

www.houseofhemp.co.uk For hemp yarns and fabrics and loads of background information.

www.organiccotton.biz If you make your own clothes, Organic Cotton has a selection of cotton plains, striped and checked cottons, calico, denim and heavy-weight jersey. All are Fairtrade too. They also sell undyed sheets and towels.

www.organicpurewool.co.uk Boasts 700 yarns all made from 100 per cent organic wool. They also sell fleece, cushions and rugs and can arrange to have garments knitted for you.

www.organicwool.co.uk DK and Aran wools from certified organic farms in Wales. They also sell blankets, throws and shawls.

www.newlanarkshop.co.uk Tweed and heather mixtures in DK and Aran.

Accessories

www.ecoaccessories.co.uk Wooden jewellery and gifts.

www.ecofibres.co.uk Good for hemp bags and accessories, as well as some hemp clothing.

www.ecofriendlybag.co.uk Canvas, jute and cotton bags.

www.exclusiveroots.com Fairtrade accessories and jewellery created by small communities in Africa.

www.ganesha.co.uk Excellent for purses, bags, scarves, wraps and flip-flops. Also sell clothing.

www.shoprecycle.co.uk Funky bags made from waste materials.

www.tinglondon.com Salvaged materials are redeployed to make belts, bags and luggage; for instance, seatbelt handbags.

www.traidcraftshop.co.uk For a good selection of Fairtrade-sourced bags and jewellery.

Jewellery

Mining for gold, silver and diamonds is hugely damaging to the environment and is threatening precarious ecosystems. Concerned environmentalists should avoid jewellery made from new, precious metals and seek out recycled jewellery in its place. **www.nodirtygold.org** gives the low-down on the various ecological and social impacts of mining for gold. There are several companies to choose from if you are looking for something special such as a wedding band or engagement ring. For everything else you could go down the non-precious route or look for antiques instead.

http://24carat.co.uk/diamondscreated.html A conventional jeweller, but has interesting information on the various types of synthetic and created diamonds.

www.credjewellery.com Trawls the world to find raw materials that have been sourced without damaging the environment or exploiting those who work in the industry. They are also active in raising awareness about the negative impact of the mining. They specialise in wedding bands and engagement rings and will make bespoke jewellery.

www.greenkarat.com They will provide you with a 'green assay', which will enable you to track the origins of the materials that have been used in your jewellery. They have a really good selection and do custom-made; however, the site is American, so you should be aware of import duties.

www.hairygrowler.co.uk Fabulous, original, 100 per cent recycled jewellery beloved of the Glastonbury Festival crowd.

www.justbazaar.co.uk A good selection of ethically-sourced jewellery including a selection of silver jewellery made in Wales. All the items have information on their origins and the materials used.

www.thebirdsinthemeadow.com Sassy, handmade jewellery made from 'recycled materials and love'.

Corporate gifts

www.freesetbags.co.uk For jute bags.

www.recycledbusinessgifts.co.uk Customised T-shirts, polos, fleeces and caps all made from recycled materials.

Facts

- We spend £23 billion on fashion annually in the UK.

- Organophosphates and organochlorines are banned in the EU but are used in cotton production in many developing countries. They cause foetal damage, nausea and headaches, and at high doses can cause death.

- A standard 100 per cent cotton T-shirt contains only 73 per cent cotton. The remainder consists of the chemicals and resins that were used to grow and make it.

- The first Levi's jeans were made from canvas ship sails, which were made entirely from hemp.

- Hemp grows up to 12 to 15 feet in 90 days.

- A single gold ring leaves in its wake around 20 tons of mine waste.

- In the Puruvian town of LaOroya, site of a smelter for the gold industry, 99 per cent of the children have severe lead poisoning.

- Three-quarters of all active mines are in areas that have been classified as being of high conservation value.

- There are 850 million workers who earn less than a living wage.

- Each year, 22,000 workers die each year due to poor working conditions.

Parenting

The internet is buzzing with information on the subject of being a good parent and it is a great resource for help with issues as and when they arise. The following sites look at the matter from an eco point of view, with the aim of both using the planet's resources wisely and developing environmentally aware offspring.

www.ecofriendlykids.co.uk Well written and researched articles on how to translate environmental concerns into practical action in the family. It covers food, products and lifestyle, recycling, school and travelling. There are also a few activities to do with the children.

www.little-green-baby.co.uk A personal site set up during pregnancy by a woman motivated to change the way she lived for the sake of her baby. There is not a huge amount of information, but the details included are written intelligently and stem from the perspective of experience.

www.thegreenparent.co.uk The *Green Lifestyle* magazine's site is designed to persuade you to subscribe to the magazine; however, there are a few articles and a lively forum.

www.treehuggermums.co.uk This is a high-quality site from TreeHugger, providing pregnancy and parenting articles principally for mums. In addition there is a blog, a shop and a good directory of links.

www.veganfamily.co.uk How to raise a vegan child with recipes, information, a blog and a good set of links.

www.vegsoc.org/info/familyindex.html A good deal of factual information on vegetarian nutrition for children.

The great nappy debate

The Environment Agency has carried out the most comprehensive study to date comparing disposable against reusable nappies. The result was the inconclusive finding that each nappy system is comparable in terms of its overall environmental impact. You can download the PDF file at **www.environment-agency.gov.uk/ commondata/acrobat/nappies_1072099.pdf.**

However, if you buy second-hand nappies, that has to tip the balance. **www.usednappies.co.uk** is an auction site devoted to doing just that.

The following are a few sites that also look at the issue. See the next section for online suppliers of nappies.

www.askbaby.com/the-nappy-debate.htm

www.ecofriendlykids.co.uk/ReUsableNappies.html

www.netmums.com/h/n/HOMELIFE/HOME/ALL/597

www.realnappycampaign.com

Breast is best

The site **www.iwantmymum.com** is put together by mums and has good information on breastfeeding.

Clothing and accessories for babies and small children

There are numerous suppliers of organic and Fairtrade children's clothes, body products, gifts and accessories; however, it is hard to find many that cater for older children and young teens.

www.bellanatura.co.uk A non-profit company that sells some African crafts and furniture along with all the baby paraphernalia and organic clothing.

www.ethical-junction.org/family/babies_children A list of links to environmental and ethically vetted sites that sell children's and baby wear.

www.green-eyed-monster.co.uk A small but trendy range of organic clothes for babies and children up to six years old.

www.mini-organic.co.uk A stylish range of organic baby clothes and organic clothing for small children.

www.naturalchild.co.uk Organic and natural products for babies and young children. The links section is good and well categorised.

www.naturalnursery.co.uk A good range of nursery products including a wide selection of nappy options, clothing, toys and slings, all posted on a nicely designed site.

www.organicchildren.com Organic toiletries and salves for babies and children, plus a few for parents too.

www.thenappylady.co.uk Fill in the detailed questionnaire and they will send you a fully costed quote. They continue to provide you with advice after you purchase the nappies.

www.underthegooseberrybush.co.uk A small but considered range for the mum-to-be and her baby.

Older children

www.calico-moon.co.uk A store catering for girls offering a few items that go up to age 13, as well as schoolwear, including summer dresses.

www.eco-eco.co.uk A reasonable range of clothing, some of which goes up to 158 centimetres.

www.gossypium.co.uk Organic, Fairtrade, cotton clothing for teens, both boys and girls. Mostly T-shirts, hoodies, soft cotton trousers and underwear. Also have clothing for younger children and adults.

www.lint-kids.com Pure, organic, school clothes suitable for eczema suffers.

www.one-world-is-enough.net Fairtrade clothes for children up to age ten.

www.peopletree.co.uk Not a huge choice, but a few cool T-shirts for teens and children plus some nice baby wear.

Shoes

www.alternativestores.com Their girls' and boys' footwear includes shoes, boots, trainers and sandals; they also have non-leather, cruelty-free dance shoes.

www.downbound.co.uk A few hemp sandals and shoes.

www.greenshoes.co.uk Vegan shoes for boys and girls. They also cater for men and women.

www.myveganshoes.com Polliwalks shoes in two styles: duck and gator.

Toys

www.escortoys.com Good-quality construction, educational, pull along and play toys manufactured in wood by employees with learning difficulties.

www.greeneyedfrog.co.uk Affordable, organic, Fairtrade and eco-friendly products and gifts for all the family including toys for children and babies.

www.georgeluckpuzzles.com Award-winning manufacturer of wooden puzzles in vibrant colours. A wide selection listed by age suitability.

www.holz-toys.co.uk Most of the products at this wonderful store originate in Germany and meet with their environmental standards. Most are wooden toys for both indoor and outdoor use, plus there are a few soft toys.

www.jumpingfrogtoys.co.uk Traditional British-made wooden toys including some timeless classics such as the bricks and turnip whip top.

www.lankakade.co.uk Fairtrade toys from Sri Lanka, many of which are made from rubberwood that is sourced from exhausted rubber plantations. Includes puzzles, board games and a few wonderful nursery clocks.

www.mulberrybush.co.uk They do not claim to be an eco supplier, but this company has a brilliant collection of traditional toys.

www.toys-to-you.co.uk An excellent toy shop with suggested toys by age, should you need inspiration. There is such a fabulous range here; you will be spoilt for choice. Shame that they cater only for little ones.

Party time

www.ecopartybags.co.uk and **www.happygreenearth.com**
enable you to fulfil your obligations with a green conscience.
There's a range of recycled and wooden gifts plus biodegradable glasses, natural starch cutlery and recycled paper plates.

Facts

● It is estimated that the ingredients for a typical Sunday lunch
  could have travelled 24,000 miles before we eat them.

● The Forestry Commission estimates that 30 per cent of the population never visit woods.

● Approximately eight million nappies are thrown away each day,
  contributing to about 4 per cent of the UK's total waste.

● Thirteen million toys end up in the dustbin and landfill sites
  every year.

● Plastic cutlery thrown away today won't fully degrade until the
  year 2508.

● Every year the average family dustbin contains enough unre-
  alised energy to power 5,000 hours of TV.

● Batteries produce 50 times less energy than it takes to make
  them.

● Children taken to school by car spend an average of two hours
  and 35 minutes in the car per week – and you can double that for
  the parent driving!

● At the peak school travel time of 8.50 a.m., nearly one in five cars
  on urban roads are taking children to school.

The young environmentalist: sites for children

The following sites are designed to entertain children while educating them about the environment. These are just the tip of the iceberg: investigate any of the links in the sites below to discover many more brilliant sites on nature, the planet and ecology.

General environmental awareness

As good place to start is with the children's pages from the Natural History Museum at **www.nhm.ac.uk/kids-only**. There are fun and games, naturecams, competitions and facts. Of course, there is the whole of the museum site to explore too, which is a fabulous nature resource in itself. The American Museum of Natural History's kids' section is also excellent – go to **www.amnh.org/ology** for a huge collection of games and activities.

Here are some more sites to inspire the kids:

http://kids.yahoo.com/science Science pages from the excellent Yahoo site for kids. There's masses to do on the site and brilliant links.

http://tolweb.org/tree/home.pages/treehouses.html An unusual site that holds a collection of information about biodiversity. The 'Treehouse' section for children has links to investigations, stories, fun and games, art and culture and webquests.

www.coolkidsforacoolclimate.com Designed to educate children about the causes and effects of climate change. The aim of the project is to engage young people and show them how they could make a difference. There is information on the International Children's Conference on the Environment too.

www.earthpeace.co.uk/Games.htm A list of educational fun and games, all with good intent, gleaned from a range of different sites.

www.ecokids.ca Educational material, fun and games are well presented on this Canadian site.

www.environment-agency.gov.uk/fun Play games, watch and interact with animations, wise up on some facts and figures, and download screensavers, all while learning about the environment.

www.foe.co.uk/learning/youth/index.html Friends of the Earth have a section devoted to young people, encouraging them to take action for the planet. There is a good links page and celebrity comment.

www.forestry.gov.uk A range of different learning opportunities, either online or out and about. There are webcams and videos to watch, and soundfiles and podcasts to listen to. You'll also find factsheets and some excellent material on climate change and forests.

www.kidsplanet.org A very American children's site with games and lots of sound effects. One for the babysitter!

www.youthagainstclimatechange.org A campaigning site aimed at motivating young people to take action against climate change. As an incentive to visit, there is a short film on the subject by Leonardo di Caprio.

Jokes for twits

Kids will love the collection of bad owl jokes from the Barn Owl Trust at **www.barnowltrust.org.uk/infopage.html?Id=186**.

Social networking

www.connect2earth.org A social networking site aimed at encouraging young people to share their thoughts on environmental issues. Pictures, videos and comments are uploaded, and then they are voted on and ranked by other visitors to the site. There's a blog too.

www.ecokids.ca/blog A Canadian site with a blog for kids.

For students, homework and teachers

Some of these sites are purely educational, while others have a high entertainment value too.

http://schools.ceh.ac.uk The Centre for Ecology and Hydrology researches and monitors terrestrial and freshwater environments and has some excellent teaching materials aimed at students and teachers. The 'basic topics' are aimed at younger children, while the information under 'advanced topics' is aimed at GCSE students. There are links too, for further investigation.

http://serc.carleton.edu/climatechange The Climate Change Collection provides 40 digital resources that are graded and reviewed for quality. Although US-orientated, there are some good resources.

www.ace.mmu.ac.uk/kids Although the Department for the Environment and Rural Affairs no longer funds this site, the information sheets and games aimed at primary school children are good. Buried in the site at **www.ace.mmu.ac.uk/resources** are further teaching resources for key stages 3 and 4, and a guide for older students. There are also links to encyclopaedias and other resources, but as the site is not updated there are no guarantees that these are all still live.

www.envision.org.uk This site links to **www.envision.uk.net**, a project set up by young people to challenge the notion that they are apathetic and disengaged. The aim is to enable 16- to 19-year-olds in schools around the country to set up their own environmental projects.

www.nceas.ucsb.edu/nceas-web/kids Kids Do Ecology: a US resource featuring material on ecology.

www.oceanservice.noaa.gov/education Great resources from the US National Oceanic and Atmospheric Administration, including 'kits' on corals, currents, tides and sea floor mapping.

www.organics.org/kids_club.php Factsheets about organic food and farming aimed at younger children.

www.wwflearning.org.uk The World Wildlife Fund is working with schools to promote sustainability. There are some excellent resources on the site and more available for purchase (mostly aimed at teachers). There is also a section entitled 'homework help' that has web field trips, project ideas, factsheets and links.

www.ypte.org.uk The Young People's Trust for the Environment has loads of animal and environmental facts, information on the scientific method, Biomes and ecolinks. You can also find out about school membership, and their talks and courses.

Earth as art

NASA's collection of stunning photographs of the planet from the Landsat-7 satellite are online at **http://earthasart. gsfc.nasa.gov**.

Wildlife

www.bbc.co.uk/nature/reallywild Quality pages from the BBC, including interactive guides to wildlife, features to discover about some of the world's most amazing habitats, plus fun and games. If that's not enough, the pages aimed at adults are brilliant for older children too.

www.rspb.org.uk/youth Pages from the RSPB encouraging children and teenagers to be interested in birds. Teens become members of 'Phoenix', which supplies them with an environmental magazine entitled *Wingbeat*. For younger children there are activities on the site, plenty of ideas for things to do with parents and some good pages devoted to learning about birds and their habitats.

www.thekidsgarden.co.uk Encouraging adults to engage children in the garden and notice the wildlife around them. There are sections on learning and planting as well as activities and a section devoted to schools.

www.wildlifewatch.org.uk An environmental action club for kids, which is sponsored by the Wildlife Trust. There is information on helping the environment, a wildlife diary, some brainteasers and ideas of things to make and do. You can also join a local group and get active.

For vegetarian young people

www.youngveggie.org With good information on what being a vegetarian means backed up by sensible advice and good, simple recipes. There are a few games and a pen pal section.

www.vegsoc.org/info/resources.html A set of links aimed at young vegetarians.

Facts

- The amount of rubbish dropped on our streets has increased by some 500 per cent since the early 1960s.

- More than 373,000 pieces of litter were found on beaches in the UK in 2006.

- There are around 30,000 invertebrate species in Britain, living on land and in our rivers and seas.

- The British Government has a target to halt the loss of wildlife by 2010.

- The average lifespan of an otter today is four years, although in ideal conditions they should live for 8 to 12 years.

Transport

The way we choose to travel is one of the biggest factors in determining our individual carbon footprint. Most means of transport are major users of oil, the burning of which produces a considerable amount of waste, including pollution and the greenhouse gas carbon dioxide.

An overview of the government's policies on transport and a plethora of information can be found at **www.dft.gov.uk** where, at the time of writing, a proposal to spend £140 million on cycle routes sat adjacent to an announcement regarding adding capacity at Heathrow; mixed messages maybe?

For a very personal take on the issues and the lack of positive action see George Monbiot's fired-up arguments on his site at **www.monbiot.com/archives/category/transport**.

Holiday travel is dealt with separately on page 159; obviously, a good deal of the information does overlap.

The car

When people talk about adopting a greener lifestyle, the car is commonly the number one issue. The freedom of the car is addictive and, for some, it is the only way that they can travel to their workplace. For many others, especially those living in the country, it is the only way to travel conveniently.

The car is particularly inefficient, especially when so often it is carrying just one person. A quarter of all journeys made by car are less than two miles; by considering our options on these journeys alone, we could considerably reduce the fuel we consume. The over-reliance on the car has brought with it the additional health burdens of obesity and asthma, and has made our towns and cities congested and dirty.

The following sites provide lots of food for thought about the type of car we drive and the options for making more environmentally considerate decisions about the way we use our car.

Environmental Transport Association

The Environmental Transport Association (**www.eta.co.uk**) aims to raise awareness of the impact of excessive car use, while providing services to car users. Profits from insurance (cycle, car, travel and home), breakdown and other services go towards its campaigns.

For environmental enlightenment, the car owner could get away with visiting only this website on the issue; it is packed with everything you could want to know. There is a car buyer's guide, which can be used to assess the green credentials of the car before you buy, then you can check the car cost calculator for the annual running costs. Under 'environmental information' there is more about buying used cars and information on the different fuels on offer. They also supply a good section on green driving tips and the organisation runs Green Transport Week. Sign up to their newsletter for regular updates.

Questions the Environmental Transport Association says you should ask about each trip:

1. Is the journey necessary?

2. Can you use a different mode of transport?

3. Can you reduce the distance with careful planning?

4. Can you drive it more efficiently?

Exploring your car's emissions

If you are interested in finding out more about the environmental impact of your car, and certainly if you are considering buying a car, check out these sites to find out more about the vehicle's emissions and environmental impact.

www.dft.gov.uk/ActOnCO2 Search for the most efficient cars in their class plus driving tips.

www.green-car-guide.com Provides independent information for car buyers about the most environmentally friendly cars to buy. You can get a list of the top ten cars and sign up for some money-saving tips online, but for the whole picture you'll have to purchase the book.

www.lowcvp.org.uk An action and advisory group aimed at the car industry with the mission to accelerate the shift to low-carbon vehicles in the UK. Look around and there are some serious reports on all vehicle types, the various fuel and hybrid options, and a searchable resources library.

www.vcacarfueldata.org.uk The Vehicle Certification Agency lists the fuel consumption, carbon dioxide and other emissions figures for new cars on the market in the UK.

Fuels

The technology that will replace the petrol and diesel engine has not yet become obvious. There is a lot of discussion about hybrid and electric cars, and natural gas or ethanol driven cars. If you are at a bit of a loss about what it is all about and how it works, you will find it clearly explained at **http://auto.howstuffworks.com/alternative-fuel-channel.htm**.

There is an ongoing debate about the benefits or otherwise of biofuels. In an attempt to cut down on greenhouse gas emissions, the government has introduced mandatory biofuel blending (2.5 per cent rising to 5 per cent in 2010). On the surface this seems like a good, green solution, but the impact of growing crops for fuel is leading to deforestation in places such as Brazil and indirectly could be accelerating climate change. Farmers are tempted to grow crops for fuel not food, which is forcing up food prices.

http://greenfuels.co.uk Amongst other things you can buy your own biodiesel processor for only £2,500! An interesting glimpse into some of the technology that is available.

http://uk.cars.yahoo.com/green-car-centre Search for a car by fuel type and read reviews on all the latest 'green' cars with loads of pictures and video clips.

www.biodieselfillingstations.co.uk For a list of garages selling biodiesel fuels.

www.lowimpact.org For factsheets on converting your car to biodiesel or vegetable oil.

www.biofuelwatch.org.uk A campaigning site packed with information and examples.

www.cbev.org and **www.evuk.co.uk** Both extol the virtues of electric vehicles.

www.dft.gov.uk/pgr/roads/environment/rtfo/biofuelsreviewtor For the government's perspective.

www.goingreen.co.uk For the G-Wiz electric car – ideal for return journeys under 48 miles.

www.hybridcars.com Information on cars using new technologies; be aware that this is an American site so the mileage will be based on US gallons not British ones (about 20 per cent difference).

www.lpgmap.co.uk Find an LPG autogas filling station or installer near you.

www.lpga.co.uk LPG autogas explained with information on filling stations in the UK and Europe.

www.organic-power.co.uk Where a sentence can contain the words 'anaerobic digestion' and 'Mercedes'. Interesting facts about biomethane and natural gas vehicles; apparently, there are over a million vehicles in Argentina, Brazil and Pakistan running on such gases already.

Cut fuel consumption by 15 per cent

The website **www.ecozone.co.uk** sells Magno Fuel devices, which fit around the fuel line of your car and embed oxygen molecules between the fuel molecules, ensuring better combustion and saving fuel.

Emission limiting driving

For a list of driving hints that will minimise your car's carbon footprint see:

www.vcacarfueldata.org.uk/information/hints-for-less-environmental-damage.asp

www.whatprice.co.uk/tips/fuel-efficiency.html

Greenmiles, embedded energy, lifecycles and greenwashing

For a thought-provoking article go to **www.worldchanging.com/archives/004425.html**.

Car clubs

Brilliant if you live in a city, particularly London, where there is no need to own a car – just book one when you need it. Go to **www.carplus.org.uk** for an interactive map and see if your locality is covered by such a scheme. **www.londoncarclubs.net** has the same information, but just for the capital.

The principle companies are:

www.citycarclub.co.uk Currently in nine cities.

www.streetcar.co.uk Great for London and beginning to establish elsewhere.

www.whizzgo.co.uk National locations, and have teamed up with Virgin trains for slick train–car connections.

Journey planning

One of the mantras is to reduce your journey's mileage and emissions with careful planning. Knowing the location of traffic blackspots and road works can reduce the time spent idling in congested traffic, which substantially cuts down on both time and wasteful fuel use. The following sites may help.

http://routeplanner.rac.co.uk Plots your route on a map showing major roadworks and duplicates this information on the route plan. You can opt for more or less motorway driving, and there is a mobile number for updates and a time range for the journey, depending on your luck with the traffic. The site has live travel news too.

www.theaa.com Check out current traffic alerts alongside a route planner. There is also a traffic blackspot warning on the directions and a phone number to call for live reports. Also alerts you to speed cameras, petrol stations, motorway services and a chain of hotels.

www.mappy.co.uk A good route planner; the beta version has traffic info.

www.multimap.com Nicely designed route planner.

Congestion charging

The introduction of congestion charging in London has resulted in:

• Twenty-one per cent less traffic entering the zone

• Forty-three per cent more cyclists

• Around 30 per cent reduction in congestion.

For more information see **www.tfl.gov.uk**.

Ride-sharing

Promote responsible car use by joining a car club. You not only help the environment but also aid congestion by sharing your journey with others. These sites help set you up with ride-share partners and provide general info on car-sharing and alternative fuels.

www.carshare.com A list of all the UK agencies that co-ordinate car shares.

www.freewheelers.com A list of lift offers, some for commuters but it's particularly good for rides to events such as festivals. Some international destinations offered.

www.liftshare.org A network of car-sharing organisations. They help you to find a match for your journey requirements.

www.nationalcarshare.co.uk A national database for ride-sharers.

www.school-run.org Part of Liftshare, helps parents find others to share the walk, cycle ride or drive to school.

The wreck

When it comes to the end of its life, we now have a duty to recycle as much of the car as possible. The government's target was to ensure that, by 2006, 85 per cent of an end of life vehicle (ELV) is recycled. **www.recycleyourcar.co.uk** will take you through the process.

www.oilbankline.org.uk Find your nearest oil bank.

www.raw2k.co.uk Buy a wreck, and then do it up or take the parts.

Motorbikes

On the face of it, using a motorbike might appear an environmentally sound option, but don't be fooled by size. There is roughly one motorbike to every 25 cars on the road; but bikes are responsible for 16 times more hydrocarbons and three times more carbon monoxide than cars; plus, they emit a selection of other toxins.

The alternative is the electric bike. In the past these have largely been scooters: very practical and ideal for some, but it has to be admitted that they have been a little short of cool. However, there are new electric motorbikes, like the Suzuki Crosscage, appearing on the market that might leave your street cred intact.

www.envbike.com Hydrogen technology makes this an almost completely clean bike. It looks good too.

www.greencarsite.co.uk/electric-bikes.htm A good collection to browse through and assess.

www.urbanmover.com Electric bikes, scooters, motorbikes, skateboards and ATVs.

Public transport

We have a love–hate relationship with public transport, but more people than ever are using it, particularly the train. When it works well, it's brilliant, but all too often trains are delayed, overcrowded and appear overpriced. If you feel let down by the public transport options, do something about it at **www.bettertransport.org.uk** – the website of a campaigning and lobbing organisation that makes sure that sustainable transport is kept on the political agenda. In addition, they support local communities in their quest for better transport links or in their fight against damaging road-building schemes.

These sites might help you use the transport system more efficiently.

www.journeyplanner.org Plan your transport route around London in a selection of languages. Options include fewest changes, fastest route and routes with the least walking between stops.

www.milesfaster.co.uk A comprehensive selection of journey planners for London and the UK for public transport or road use.

www.rail.co.uk A portal for sites associated with the railways, including travel updates, timetables and ticketing.

www.seat61.com A very personal approach to travelling by train. The man in seat 61 will tell you the best routes, provide timetables and demystify the pass system, whether you wish to travel to Paris, Hungary, Cambodia or New Zealand. There is information about the boats you'll need too.

www.transportdirect.info An excellent journey planner integrating rail, bus, car and flight information. Type in your start and end point and the site will list the options, including the estimated time for the journey, so you can compare the train, coach and car journeys side by side. You can calculate your fuel cost and carbon dioxide emissions too. The city-to-city quick planner is particularly good at comparing travel options. There is park and ride info and live travel news as well. A good site to bookmark for the PDA.

www.traveline.org.uk Here you can instantly plan your journey anywhere in the UK, either locally or long distance, using public transport, with details of times and connections.

www.travelmole.com/stories/1123984.php For an article on the relative carbon costs of flying versus coach travel.

Travel plans

www.acttravelwise.org A newly formed organisation that wants to have 'a serious impact on the harmful effects of transport' by providing a database of information to those responsible for travel plans. Their 'press watch' also provides transport-related articles from the media.

Integrated ticketing

Find out how to buy your bus ticket with your train ticket at **www.plusbus.info**. Unfortunately, there is no online sales facility yet.

Cycling

The most cost-effective and beneficial means of transport is the bicycle. Many of our towns and cities are putting cycle paths in place to make this a safer and more pleasant option than in the past. The Sustrans site listed below has details. In addition, contact your local council for information on the routes in your area – if there are none, there is bound to be a campaign group aiming to set routes up, so join. For recreational cycling there are a number of long-distance cycle ways; again, Sustrans has the information. If you like the idea of cycling but find it too energetic, then compromise with an electric bike.

www.50cycles.com A good selection of electric bikes for recreation and commuting.

www.bikeforall.net/linkcat.php Bikeforall has an excellent resource bank and is useful for commuters and leisure cyclists, as well as biking the school run.

www.ctc.org.uk The UK's largest cyclists' organisation has masses of information and a route mapping database, which is great for planning longer trips.

www.cycleweb.co.uk A general all-round resource for the cyclist.

www.lcc.org.uk A cycling campaign group aiming to make London a world-class cycling city. Their site has some interesting information. You can join in their campaigns and go for a ride.

www.nationaltrail.co.uk Details on over 25,000 miles of cycling, walking and riding trails with related features and fabulous photos.

www.saferoutestoschools.org.uk The Sustrans site that is working to make cycling to school a safe and enjoyable option.

www.sustrans.org.uk There is excellent information for cyclists, including details on the National Cycle Network and long distance cycling, commuting advice and the *Guardian* cycling guide.

www.tfl.gov.uk/roadusers/cycling/972.aspx London Transport has good information about cycling in the city, including cycling guides and a cycling journey planner.

Flying

As a prosperous nation, we have become accustomed to cheap air travel and are increasingly taking short-haul mini breaks in addition to our annual holiday. As a result, British international aviation emissions rose 1.5 per cent in 2006 alone. While the principal greenhouse gas emission from aircraft is carbon dioxide, other greenhouse gases that are emitted from planes produce a global warming effect 2.7 times greater than carbon dioxide alone (according to the Intergovernmental Panel on Climate Change). High altitude airlines travelling in or near the stratosphere are thought to make a more significant contribution to climate change than those flying at lower altitudes, with vapour trails causing a particularly harmful effect.

http://en.wikipedia.org/wiki/Aviation_and_the_environment has a good synopsis of the science. To calculate the emissions for a given flight, go to **www.climatecare.org/calculators/flight**. More offset sites are given on page 21. Other issues such as noise and airport expansion are also covered in the following sites.

www.airportwatch.org.uk and **www.planestupid.com** Both sites are against unsustainable airport expansion and excessive flying.

www.lowflyzone.org A blogging and picture site where you can find out what other people are doing to reduce their impulse to fly. You can also take the 'Lowflyzone pledge'.

www.sustainableaviation.co.uk An industry site setting out a long-term strategy for sustainability in the UK airline industry.

Shipping

Recent research suggests that the impact of shipping on climate change has been underestimated and that shipping is emitting greenhouse gases at nearly twice the rate of aviation. The old calculations put the output at 600 million tons (aviation is estimated at 650 million tons), but it is now thought to be nearer to one billion tons and growing at a rate of 4.5 per cent annually. Anyone who has watched ferries leaving port, belching black, odorous smoke, would not doubt this to be true. This is a compelling reason for carefully monitoring consumption of overseas products, including foodstuffs, as 90 per cent of global trade relies on shipping.

Oil and its derivates also pollute the oceans. Much of this is down to shipping and not just exhaust emissions. Ship-to-ship refuelling and the washing out of tanks are thought to be particularly damaging to marine environments. The Marine Conservation Society's website at **www.mcsuk.org** has more information and is a really interesting read.

The legacy of the Exxon Valdez

This factsheet looks at the cost to human health and the marine environment 15 years on: **www.akaction.org/ fact_sheets/Exxon_Valdez_Oil_Spill_Legacy_Fact_Sheet.**

---

http://en.wikipedia.org/wiki/Ship_pollution A comprehensive overview.

http://green.ferrycheap.com Encourages ferry passengers to add a contribution when booking to mitigate their carbon emissions.

Facts

- If everyone in the UK drove at 70 miles per hour max we would save one million tons of carbon dioxide every year.

- The fastest-growing source of carbon dioxide in Britain is transport; its emissions increased by 50 per cent between 1990 and 2002.

- People make 45 per cent more trips by train than ten years ago.

- By 2050 aviation will account for more than 15 per cent of worldwide carbon dioxide levels.

- In the past ten years the real cost of driving has fallen by 10 per cent, while the cost of taking the train has increased by 6 per cent and taking the bus by 13 per cent!

- In 20 years' time, experts predict that there will be 30 per cent more cars on the road – 5.7 million more than in 2007.

- Fifty-eight per cent of the population claim to consider the environment when purchasing a new car.

- Seventy-five per cent of people live within two miles of the National Cycle Network.

- One in four car journeys are a bike-friendly ride of two miles or less.

- You can travel four times faster on a bike than you walk while using the same amount of energy.

- Aviation generates nearly as much carbon dioxide in one year as the total population of Africa.

- Only 2 per cent of children cycle to school.

- Between 1990 and 2004 the number of people using airports in the UK rose by 120 per cent. As a consequence, carbon dioxide emissions almost doubled in that period, from 20.1 to 39.5 million tons.

- In heavy traffic jams the air quality can be poorer inside the car than out. Car users are regularly exposed to three times as much pollution as pedestrians.

Travel and tourism

Eco travel is a growth area in the travel industry and many firms are getting on the bandwagon, so be particularly careful about 'greenwashing'. There is no single green certification programme in the travel industry, but there are a number of inspection and accreditation schemes, so be sure that the holiday you choose is endorsed by one with a rigorous vetting procedure, not one to which companies simply pay a fee to be listed.

General info

A good all-round starting point is the *Guardian's* Green Travel pages at **www.guardian.co.uk/travel/green**, which have a searchable assortment of holiday ideas and related information. For more thought-provoking articles on eco-travel and associated themes try **www.ecotravelling.co.uk**, which explores issues such as selecting a hotel, modes of transport and holiday ideas.

Our section on transport (page 146), where the perils of the aviation industry, the car culture and public transport are explored in more detail, should be considered in conjunction with these listings. There are also a number of carbon offsetting schemes in the 'Climate change' section on page 21.

www.ecoescape.org A website and guide series that promotes environmentally friendly holidays in the UK and Ireland. They really want you to buy their books, but there are some good features and shared readers' experiences on the site.

www.tourismconcern.org.uk A UK-based charity that fights exploitation in tourism worldwide. They campaign to eradicate unregulated tourism development, which is 'destroying environments, degrading cultures and diverting essential resources'. See their section aimed at tourists for advice.

Eco travel specialists

http://ecobookers.com The eco wing of ebookers, this is a reliable travel site for independent travellers. They will help you book eco-friendly accommodation around the world, backed up with some advice on how to be a responsible tourist. They offer good prices on flights and will arrange for carbon offsetting.

http://ecofriendlytourist.com A good starting point for UK-based travellers with holiday ideas, places to stay, plus information and links to tour operators and public transport sites. There are links to some great articles and travel book reviews.

www.ecoafrica.com African specialists who check that trips and establishments listed on their website comply to minimum environmental standards. Those that meet all their criteria are given their ecoQuest seal.

www.ecoclub.com The International Tourism Club site is worth a look. They have a small selection of ecologically friendly hotels and holidays, but their strength is in their listings and the information aimed at professionals, including a magazine, job listings, a forum and education section. You need to join to get the best out of the site.

www.ecoescape.org A growing green travel guide and online directory of environmentally friendly places to stay at and visit in the UK.

www.ecotravel.com An easy-to-use search facility enables you to track down a wide range of independent hotels and tour companies with good credentials. There is also a magazine for inspiration and book reviews.

www.ecotourism.org Website of the International Ecotourism Society, a well-established American eco tourism organisation that has a mission to promote sustainable travel. Look under 'travel choice' for a guide to responsible travelling and an eco-trip search engine.

www.friendsofworldheritage.org Book a trip to one of the UN's World Heritage Sites through them (via Expedia) and the profits from your trip will go back to the Friends of the World Heritage Fund.

www.responsibletravel.com Probably the best eco holiday site with a large selection of organised and tailor-made holidays from a reputable British company. Many trips have itineraries for special interest groups, including holidays suitable for families, honeymooners and seniors, and trips for cyclists, sailors and bird lovers.

Responsible Tourism Awards

Check out the winners at **www.responsibletourismawards. com**.

Just hotels

There are a number of emerging sites in this area, but few have a wide selection of destinations on offer.

www.environmentallyfriendlyhotels.com An American site with a worldwide listing of hotels.

www.itsagreengreenworld.com A nicely designed British site but with a limited offer.

www.naturalretreats.com/locations.html Luxury accommodation in the British countryside.

Campsites

Both **www.ukcampsite.co.uk** and **www.uk-sites.com** search for campsites by name, town or county.

Working holidays

This is another growth area. Many people no longer want to travel for the sake of it, but wish to give something back to host communities or to share their skills in the poorer parts of the planet. Beware the trip that is profit-making for the organiser, but has a poor attitude towards the beneficiaries and fails to deliver a worthwhile experience for yourself. Do the background research and try to find others that have used their services. See also the section on volunteering on page 175.

http://ecofriendlytourist.com/volunteering.aspx For advice and links.

www.coralcay.org Contribute to Coral Cay Conservation projects for as little as one week. You can be trained to dive or be a qualified diver; alternatively, you can work on a land-based project. It isn't an inexpensive option, but it costs considerably less if you are in a group of six or more. They have a good ethical and environmental policy and are endorsed by their president, Professor David Bellamy.

www.ecovolunteer.com Give your services to a specific animal benefit project from wild horses in Mongolia to humpback whales in Brazil.

www.ethicalvolunteering.org A great starting point for someone wanting to volunteer for a short trip or a gap year, with information on how to select organisations that will truly make use of your skills and benefit the people or environments that you are hoping to work for.

www.responsibletravel.com This site has over 300 tailor-made and small-group volunteer holidays.

Facts

- **In four out of five countries tourism is one on the top five industries.**

- **By 2020 it is expected that there will be in the region of 1.56 billion international arrivals worldwide.**

- **Out of 109 countries with coral reefs, 90 report damage due to cruise ships, sewage or harvesting for souvenirs.**

- **Tourism is the most important earner of foreign exchange in one-third of the world's poorest nations.**

- **According to a recent poll, Scotland was the number one eco tourism destination in Europe.**

- **Eighty per cent of tourists say that they are prepared to pay extra to stay in environmentally friendly accomodation.**

- **The greatest environmental impacts from tourism are caused by air travel.**

- Nineteen per cent of UK adults report they are already taking, or plan to take, more holidays in the UK as a response to environmental concerns.

- The paved area of a large airport such as Heathrow is the equivalent of 200 miles of three-lane motorway.

- Buses and coaches account for only 1 per cent of the total vehicle mileage on Britain's roads.

- Every week a cruise ship creates 210,000 gallons of sewage and 37,000 gallons of oily bilge water!

Days out

The following are a few suggestions for ways to spend your down time while feeling that you are learning more about the natural world or simply getting out and appreciating it. In order to make your journey as environmentally efficient as possible, check out the options at **www.transportdirect.info**.

Events listings and festivals

http://greenfuturesfestivals.org.uk Along with information about the Green Futures Festivals, there is a good events listing covering everything from the Anarchist Bookfair to Womad.

www.big-green-gathering.com Claims to be Europe's biggest green festival with music, exhibitions, crafts, food and numerous other activities. It is held at Glastonbury and attracts around 20,000 participants.

www.camdengreenfair.org.uk Camden's free green fair and bikefest.

www.ecological-living.co.uk/page.php/events For a small events listing including exhibitions and eco-themed charity runs.

www.guardian.co.uk/environment/series/greenagenda Has a good events listing for green-themed debates, festivals, art projects, campaigns and activities.

Forests

www.communityforest.org.uk There are 12 community forests in England; find out about these on the interactive map. You will be directed to the forest of your choice where you can find out about walking trails and events such as family and planting days.

www.forestry.gov.uk Has interactive maps that enable you to locate Forestry Commission woodland suitable for walking, cycling or horse riding. The maps can also be used to find out if there are any events planned in individual forests and which forests are suitable for activities such as camping, fishing or watersports.

www.woodland-trust.org.uk Look under 'our woods' to find a searchable directory of over 1,000 woods, with interactive mapping and pictures of the woods themselves.

Walking, cycling and wildlife watching

www.aonb.org.uk The National Association for Areas of Outstanding Natural Beauty has information about visiting these special places. Select the area of your choice and you will be directed to their website.

www.blueflag.org Look under 'Blue Flag beaches and marinas' in the menu and find out where the cleanest beaches are in England, Scotland, Wales and Ireland (and in each EU county as well).

www.cnp.org.uk The umbrella site for National Parks. The map shows the location of the parks followed by contact information for each one, including a hyperlink. **www.scnp.org.uk** is the equivalent Scottish site.

www.countrysiderecreation.com A site encouraging access to the countryside in Northern Ireland. Under 'activities' there are links to Outdoor Northern Ireland, Ecotrails and sites dedicated to walking, cycling, canoeing and horse riding.

www.go4awalk.com This busy and unwieldy site boasts of having 13,500 fantastic walks and walking ideas. You have to join to get access to the downloadable maps and route information.

www.nationaltrail.co.uk National Trails comprise 15 long-distance walking cycling and horse riding routes in England and Wales. In Scotland there are four such trails called long-distance routes. Find out about them here.

www.naturalengland.org.uk Select a region from the map and you will be given the chance to see a list of events such as farm demonstrations, guided walks or talks. The interactive map allows you to search for nature reserves, Sites of Special Scientific Interest (SSSI), Biodiversity Action Plan priority habitats, agri-environment schemes and geological sites.

www.onedayhikes.com Has a selection of one-day hikes around the world complete with detailed trail descriptions and notes on the walk; unfortunately, there are no maps.

www.ramblers.org.uk Has everything you need to know as a walker in Britain. There is information on where to go, and how to join an organised walk and other Ramblers' activities.

www.rspb.org.uk Visit one of the 200 nature reserves run by the RSPB. You can find out where they are located, and about scheduled events and activities and the facilities that you will find when you get there.

www.snh.org.uk Working to protect Scottish natural heritage, this site has information about the National Nature Reserves. In the section called 'wimby' (what's in my back yard) you can search for information including RSPB and Wildlife Trust reserves, local reserves, local groups and societies.

www.sustrans.org.uk The Sustainable Transport charity has information on the National Cycling Network as well as information on rides and events.

www.walkingworld.com Features 4,000 walks worldwide, but you have to subscribe to the site or buy the map and details.

www.waterscape.com For boating, fishing, cycling and walking along Britain's 4,000 miles of waterways. The search engine helps you locate the activities on offer.

www.wildlifetrusts.org Visit one of their nature reserves or participate in one of their organised activities.

www.wildlifewatching.org The People's Trust for Endangered Species organise wildlife-watching opportunities throughout the country. These trips enable you to meet the conservationists and learn about the Trust's projects to help endangered animals. You can sign up online.

www.wwt.org.uk The Wildfowl and Wetlands Trust (WWT) is a leading UK conservation organisation dedicated to saving wetlands. They have nine sites in the UK to visit.

Museums and science

www.cat.org.uk The Centre for Alternative Technology in central Wales makes an inspiring day out. The eco centre is full of interactive displays and practical examples on how to make life more sustainable.

www.culture24.org.uk Has the news, listings and features from 3,000 museums and heritage sites in the UK. It is a bit hard to find what you are looking for on this vast site. Try typing in the town or country you are interested in and the search engine does a pretty good job at finding the relevant pages. The 'what's on' section is good and easy to use.

www.edenproject.com Explore man's relationship with plants at this marvellous science park, containing over one million plants representing 5,000 species. Some of the plants are outdoors while others are located in the biodomes – giant conservatories; one devoted to humid, tropical plants; the other representing a warm temperate zone. It is 'unashamedly entertaining' but boasts of its academic excellence and scientific integrity.

www.museums.co.uk Here you can search the database of museums by keyword, location or using the interactive map.

Zoos, safari parks and aquaria

http://myweb.tiscali.co.uk/zoodirectory An extensive alphabetical and regional listing of all the major zoos, aquaria and marine parks, bird centres, butterfly centres and safari parks in the UK. The site is pretty basic but it's functional and the hyperlinks work.

www.safaripark.co.uk A listing of safari parks in the UK with hyperlinks to take you directly to their sites. There is also great background information about the animals and the experience to get the family excited about the visit.

Gardens

www.farmgarden.org.uk Representing city farms, community gardens and allotments. Look under 'farms and gardens' to locate one in the city you are visiting. They have also become involved in local food and sustainable community initiatives.

www.gardenvisit.com This site lists over 2,260 gardens worldwide as well as over 600 nurseries. Use the garden finder to narrow down your search. You'll find information and interactive mapping links to each garden's website, and they can also help you find accommodation in the area.

www.greatbritishgardens.co.uk A similar garden site to gardenvisit.com, but with a different listing of wonderful gardens to visit in the UK.

www.nationaltrust.org.uk The National Trust is involved in a great deal of conservation work. You can read about it on their site before going to visit one of their properties. There are costal and countryside locations as well as gardens and heritage buildings.

www.ngs.org.uk The National Garden Scheme publishes the 'Yellow Book' of gardens open to the public for charity. Most of the gardens are privately owned and are opened for just a day or two per year. They present a marvellous opportunity to visit these gardens nurtured by enthusiasts. You can search by postcode, garden name or county. **www.gardensofscotland.org** runs a similar scheme for Scotland.

Facts

- Seventy-eight per cent of all journeys under one mile are made on foot.

- Only 20 per cent of people in the UK currently get enough exercise to maintain a healthy lifestyle. Walking at a reasonable pace for 30 minutes, five times a week is a good way to meet this target.

- There are 4,000 miles of waterways in Britain.

- In one year, 106 million visitor days were spent in the National Parks of England.

- In England and Wales there are around 2,500 miles of National Trail pathways.

- In the past three years 16 species that are new to Britain have been observed on RSPB nature reserves.

- Freshwater wetlands are home to more than 40 per cent of the world's known species, including 12 per cent of all animal species.

- In the 1960s rhino populations were estimated at 100,000; today, this number has reduced to about 13,000.

The workplace

The workplace places a huge drain on planetary resources but the effects can be minimised with less of a detrimental effect on daily routines, business practices and the bottom line than many company directors imagine. There are clear benefits too in terms of the public perception of a business that has taken steps to become green. As an introduction, many questions are answered by way of video clips at **www.videojug.com/tag/green-product-design**.

A good deal of the information in this section is also relevant to the home office, including personal computers and associated paraphernalia. Business solutions to global warming are also covered by a section under climate change on page 24, while there is more about energy on page 50 and recycling on page 58.

Greening the workplace

There are a number of internet resources that can point a business in the right direction and make a start on greening the workplace.

www.choosethealternative.co.uk This company will provide you with a sustainability 'Smartcheck' to analyse your current business practices. They will then work with you to come up with strategies and help you achieve your set goals.

www.envirowise.gov.uk A government-funded service offering 'free independent, confidential advice and support on practical ways to increase profits, minimise waste and reduce environmental impact'. The advice comes by way of an advice line, case study and other reference materials, and over 200 events per year. They also offer an on-site visit.

www.goitgreener.com For advice on making the greenest choices when it comes to computer equipment and technology. They also offer virtual help in writing and implementing a green policy for businesses.

www.greenconsumerguide.com/commercial.php A great resource that publishes news stories and provides background information on issues that relate to business. They list headline stories on the front page, but you can also check for information under the 16 categories that include finance, IT solutions and waste. To keep yourself updated, you can have news fed to you on your WAP or as a newsfeed; alternatively, you could sign up to their newsletter.

www.greenplanetpr.co.uk A PR agency that undertakes to get your environmental credentials to work for you.

Office stationery and supplies

Look for the NAPM (**www.napm.org.uk**) or the Eugropa Recycled Mark when buying paper. These are awarded to papers that contain a minimum of 75 per cent genuine waste.

http://ecotopia.co.uk A comprehensive office supplier offering everything from envelopes, a staple-less stapler, low-energy PCs and media players to water-powered calculators and recycled toilet rolls.

http://rps.gn.apc.org Recycled stationery, art and craft materials and reuse labels. They also supply custom-printed promotional products.

www.elliepoopaper.co.uk For something a little bit different – 100 per cent recycled, chemical-free, chlorine-free, acid-free, machine and hand-made paper with a number of curious additions, including elephant or rhino poo, rose petals, coffee and more besides.

www.greenstat.co.uk The Green Stationery Company selects products that are 'environmentally benign or have environmental advantages over the standard stationery equivalents'. They have a good range of products from printer paper to a wind-up mobile phone charger.

www.newleafpaper.com Paper made from ultra-high, post-consumer waste and non-wood fibres, free from chlorine and bleach.

www.remarkableoffice.co.uk This company began life in the quest to turn a plastic cup into a pencil. They have gone on to make a wide range of products, many of which can be personalised. They also sell the usual office supplies (green, of course) such as paper, cleaning products and water-based markers and well as their inspired recycled range.

Computing

Computers use massive amounts of energy in the workplace and at home. If you are interested in keeping up to date and learning more about the issues you may be interested in **www.computing. co.uk/knowledge/green**, where there's an excellent section devoted to green computing. There is also a forum if you want to chat about it. For more on recycling old computers, see page 63. The following companies offer a more responsible and sustainable approach to IT.

www.climatesaverscomputing.org An American site encouraging manufacturers, business and individuals to demand more energy-efficient computers. They will guide you through the energy management system on your PC. There is also a product catalogue full of smarter computing-related products, although they do not sell from the site.

www.green-computer-services.co.uk Comes at the subject from a slightly different angle, being primarily concerned with the reduction of waste and, where possible, the recycling and reuse of products and materials. They sell a range of green computers that are not only energy saving, but made from recyclable materials. They supply refurbished computers and offer computer repairs. They also help to dispose of your old computers.

www.ethiscore.org/reports/free/computers_desktop.aspx Advice from a non-profit organisation that assesses the companies behind the brand names and scores them out of 20. They also tag them for their environmental credentials.

www.very-pc.co.uk This company won the Environmental Innovator category in the PC Pro Awards in 2007, so they are worth checking out. They specialise in energy-efficient PCs, servers and IT infrastructures, and offer hardware, consultancy, support and internet services. They also supply a range of home computers.

www.zerocarbonfootprint.co.uk Offers a green low-energy PC where carbon dioxide is offset by tree-planting campaigns. They claim to reduce electricity costs from computer usage by almost 70 per cent.

Ideas for an ethical surfer

This *Guardian* article has several ideas on how to make good ethical use of your time on the net: **www.guardian.co.uk/ technology/2000/nov/16/internetnews.onlinesupplement1**.

Web and design

The following are web and graphic design companies that specialise in the green and sustainable sector.

www.ethos.uk.net

www.sustainabledesign.co.uk

www.thedesignpod.net

www.luminair.co.uk In addition to graphic and web design, they offer 'unique, environmentally conscious products, bespoke designs and commissions and energy efficient lighting design and a consultancy service'.

www.wordetc.co.uk An environmentally aware editorial and design company that works mainly in the non-profit and charity sector. They will advise on making responsible decisions with regard to printing and publishing.

Hosting and ISP

www.greenwebhost.net Another green web-hosting service and it also provides a green broadband ISP for both office and home.

www.greenisp.net Named as the 'best buy' in *Ethical Consumer* magazine's ISP special, this ISP offers home and business broadband and dial-up services. The company is non-profit and their offices are solar powered and carbon neutral.

www.lightbeingcreations.co.uk and **www.solarhost.co.uk** Both are energy-efficient, solar-powered, web-hosting companies. The former also offers web design. Using this technology enables users of the service to make the claim that their websites do not harm the environment.

Advertising and marketing

www.blueginger.co.uk A marketing, PR and advertising agency that describes itself as 'a cool shade of leaf green'.

www.dogoodadvertising.com Works only on projects that are in line with their own ethical standards.

www.feelagency.com An ethical marketing agency with a cool and original website.

www.theethicalagency.co.uk An advertising agency that will only work with ethical businesses.

Fairtrade

Signing up to the Fairtrade initiative is another marker of an ethical company. **www.videojug.com/tag/fair-trade** again answers the obvious questions and includes a section on the business side of Fairtrade. For more information about Fairtrade visit the Foundation's site at **www.fairtrade.org.uk**, where there is a section devoted to business services. This includes information about getting products certified, how to register as a supplier and how to source Fairtrade goods.

Careers and jobs

The following sites offer career information to those who think that they might want a career in the ethical or environmental sector.

www.britishecologicalsociety.org The British Ecological Society has a good introduction to careers in ecology.

www.ethicalcareersguide.co.uk With news, features, real-life accounts, a career doctor, virtual careers fair, web directory and book shop, this site provides a huge amount of material to be browsed by anyone looking for inspiration or wanting to find out more about a chosen career.

www.greendirectory.net Good for news updates, jobs, courses and events nationwide. They also have a portal on green theses, where graduate, masters and doctorate theses can be posted and made accessible to the public.

A number of sites have searchable databases of environmental jobs. Most of these companies cover all industry sectors:

http://jobs.guardian.co.uk

www.biggreenswitch.co.uk/jobs

www.eco-uk.com/jobgroup.cfm (ecological jobs)

www.endsjobsearch.co.uk

www.environmentalcareers.org.uk

www.environmentpost.co.uk

www.ethical-jobs.co.uk

www.greenenergyjobs.com (energy sector)

www.greenjobsonline.co.uk

www.guidemegreen.com/jobs

Volunteering

Volunteering can be a fulfilling activity in itself, or can be a stepping stone for a career. The following sites can give you a steer.

www2.btcv.org.uk The British Trust for Conservation volunteers runs a wide range of activities from days out to holidays. The site also features their 'green gyms', which have attracted publicity as a way of keeping fit while doing something useful; if there's not one near you, then there is encouragement for you to start one.

www.greenguide.co.uk Has a section 'eco volunteers' which lists current opportunities both in the UK and abroad.

www.onlinevolunteering.org A UN site that connects volunteers and development organisations over the internet. When we visited there were over 150 different opportunities available on the site, from moderating a consultation on youth migration to working as a geographical consultant on a conservation project, all from the comfort of your home.

www.volstudy.ac.uk The University of Wales, Lampeter offers a distance learning Certificate in Interpersonal Skills for Volunteers. They also offer a BA in Volunteer Studies.

www.volunteering.org.uk The Volunteer England site aims to inspire more people to become volunteers. There is advice on how to volunteer in your own community, in the UK or overseas, and a section covering information about becoming an environmental or conservation volunteer. There are also volunteer blogs to read. The site provides general facts on volunteering (both for the volunteer and the managers of volunteers), an e-zine and links.

www.wildlifetrusts.org This umbrella organisation for the various local trusts relies on volunteers for much of its development and maintenance work. The site has a 'volunteers' section that lists the volunteering opportunities nationally. Check out your local trust as there may well be other activities available to you on these sites.

www.wwv.org.uk Worldwide Volunteering is a non-profit organisation that has projects for anyone who can give a week, a month or a year. They have a searchable database of organisations to help you find your match, a good deal of background material and volunteers' personal stories.

A portal for environmental careers

www.environmentcareers.org.uk is a great place to start if you think that you would be interested in a greener career, with signposts for jobs, placements, courses, work experience and volunteering.

Facts

- In the UK 750,000 tons of short-life office paper is used annually; 75 per cent of this is imported and 90 per cent is thrown away.

- A PC used for eight hours in a working day can consume 200 to 300 watts of power, even when power-saving modes are enabled; the resulting annual emissions are almost 220 kilograms of carbon dioxide.

- If counties agreed to take action on climate change now, it would cost just 1 per cent of the global gross domestic product. Failure to do so could shrink the global economy by 20 per cent.

- Twenty-four per cent of global emissions are related to power.

- Leaving a photocopier on overnight uses enough energy to print more than 1,500 A4 pieces of paper.

- Turning down the thermostat by one degree can reduce the heating bill of typical office by 10 per cent a year.

- The average office worker uses about one tree's worth of paper each year.

- Switching off lighting when not in use could save nearly 20 per cent on lighting costs.

- The production of chips needed to power one computer results in around 40 kilograms of waste. The manufacture of the circuit board (weighing about 1.8 kilograms) can produce 21 kilograms of waste, 18 kilograms of which are classified as hazardous.

● **The standard computer wastes around 50 per cent of the power delivered to it.**

● **The average UK citizen will produce approximately 3.3 tons of WEEE (waste electrical and electronic equipment) in their lifetime – the equivalent of 160 mobile phones.**

● **Waste typically costs companies 3.4 per cent of their annual turnover; 25 per cent of this waste can be easily avoided in most offices.**

Finance

For most of us it is now impractical to keep our money under the mattress. Whether it is the mortgage, rent or utilities to pay, it is generally assumed that we will have a bank account – some companies even charge us more should we have the audacity to wish to use cash. And this is just the start. We deal with other financial institutions when it comes to arranging a pension or a car insurance policy. If there is money to spare, there are savings to keep, investments to make or shares to buy.

What the banks and financial institutions do with our money should be of concern to everyone. The political and financial power of the finance sector cannot be under-estimated. As consumers we have the opportunity to send a strong message to these institutions by buying products that have good ethical and green credentials, and avoiding investments in companies and regimes that are exploitative of their environment, their workforce or the wider community.

The finance sector has responded to consumer pressure and is now offering a wider range of products to choose from. But be aware that their green credentials cover quite a broad spectrum; from dark green – those with the strictest and most restrictive policies; to a pale shade of light green – those that that allow for more flexibility. The following provide some leads, but as with all financial products it is always advisable to do some homework before making a financial commitment.

How green is your investment?

When comparing green financial products, these are the sorts of considerations that you should look for in their policies.

Dark green investment policies are generally based on the following criteria:

- Negative screening – a list of practices that are unacceptable; for example, screening out the tobacco, armament or pesticide industries.

- Cause-based investment – investing in companies for social and environmental betterment; for example, organic farming or Fairtrade companies.

Light green investment policies are generally based on:

- Positive screening – investing in companies that demonstrate a number of criteria such as recycling, good employment credentials or sound environmental policies.

- Best of sector – investing in the companies within a sector that demonstrate the highest standards; for example, chemical companies with the best environmental policy and track record. The idea is to motivate other companies to compete on their green credentials.

- Positive engagement – supporting businesses who undertake to fulfil environmental or ethical conditions; for example, in the fashion sector, guaranteeing to audit and improve working conditions and agreeing a percentage use of recycled or organic materials.

Independent financial advice

The average consumer is well advised to seek the help of an IFA (Independent Financial Advisor) to assess the suitability of a product for his or her needs, while selecting one which is likely to be a sound investment. Be sure to ask the IFA for information on the companies and sectors that any individual fund invests in and the percentage of the fund that is actually used for ethical investment. The range may surprise you.

www.eiris.org Ethical Investment Research Services is probably the best place to start your research on ethical finance. There is a wealth of advice on this site for the private individual as well as companies, charities and those working in the finance sector. In the 'personal finance' section there is information about ethical investment funds, shares, pensions, mortgages, insurance, banking and advisors. They are not authorised to give financial advice; however, they do provide you with a number of questions to ask a financial advisor about his credentials before you sign up.

www.ethicalinvestors.co.uk With nearly 20 years in this business they are able to give good ethical advice and, as they give 50 per cent of their profits to charities and good causes, they seem to be of sound credentials themselves. They have a good section explaining, in some depth, the nature of ethical investment in the different sectors. They also compare different products. If you fill in their contact form stating the nature of the advice you are looking for, they will put you in touch with suitable IFAs, who are members of their organisation, in your area.

www.ethicalscreening.com Undertakes research and analysis of the non-financial aspects of corporate activity; that is, how companies deal with their stakeholder groups including employees and the communities in which they operate.

www.greenconsumerguide.com Another source of good background information on green financial matters.

www.holden-partners.co.uk Has an excellent downloadable guide to climate change investment. There is background information and an investment comparison chart, which lists the investment funds, where the assets are held and the percentage held in environmental stocks (which, when stated, seemed surprisingly modest).

www.uksif.org A 'membership network that promotes sustainable and responsible financial services'. It is worth looking at their site to see the range of concerns that they address. They have a separate site aimed at consumers (**www.investability.org**), which is designed to help individuals understand and assess green and ethical investments.

In the news

Keep abreast of ethical money matters with the *Guardian's* Ethical Money pages at **www.guardian.co.uk/money/ ethicalmoney**.

Banking

If you are not sure how socially responsible your bank is, a visit to **www.banktrack.org** will be illuminating. They track the operations of the private financial sector, expose activities that are considered to be against the principles of social responsibility and provide details of bad deals.

The following banks have a good track record in ethical banking:

www.co-operativebank.co.uk The most ethical of the mainstream banks, offering insurance and other financial products too. The bank bases its ethical policy on the concerns of its customers, who are kept regularly updated on projects.

www.charitybank.org Links people who would like to have a deposit account that benefits society with organisations that have excellent charitable or sustainable objectives.

www.ecology.co.uk The Ecology Building Society is a mutual society that promotes the concept of sustainability through mortgage lending and a range of ethical savings accounts.

www.triodos.co.uk Triodos Bank only lends money to ethical ventures. For instance, their saver account will directly link your savings with organisations that benefit people and the environment.

Miscellaneous financial sites

www.climatesure.co.uk Car and travel insurance with carbon offsets built in.

www.fairpensions.org.uk Calls for responsible investment by UK pension funds by promoting ethical investment and sustainable development. They suggest ways in which you can add your voice.

www.ftse.com Look up the 'ftse4good' index, a share index for socially responsible investors. Some companies offer a tracker plan to this index.

www.naturesave.co.uk Offers general insurance products (travel, home, personal accident and illness) and 10 per cent of its premiums go towards environmental and conservationist projects.

Join LETS

If all this talk about money is unappealing, join LETS. Local Exchange Trading Schemes are local community-based, mutual aid networks in which people exchange all kinds of goods and services with one another, without the need for money. Check out **www.letslinkuk.net**.

Facts

- **Fifty-six per cent of consumers surveyed by the *Green Consumer Guide* said that they would object to investing in companies that break environmental regulations.**

- **In 2001 97 per cent of Co-operative Bank customers who responded to their survey supported the principle of ethical banking.**

- **FTSE4Good Index tracks the performance of companies that 'meet globally recognised corporate responsibility standards'.**

- **According to a study by Holden and Partners, only one out of 58 ethical funds surveyed claimed to have more than 50 per cent of its portfolio in environmental stocks. So take the time to read portfolios.**

- **In 2006 around £6 billion was invested in around 60 funds investing on socially responsible principles.**

Disclaimer

We've got to say it – these pages are written for information purposes only. The Green Website Guide *does not purport to be an expert in financial matters, nor is it giving financial advice.*

Pets

Put your pooch on the same footing as your family with these natural, organic and vegetarian/vegan online pet shops and pet food sites.

General petshops

www.animalpure.co.uk This company has an own-brand range of natural, organic and eco-friendly dog and cat accessories, including hemp dog collars, loofah cat toys and eco dog baskets made from hemp and stuffed with a lining made from recycled plastic bottles.

www.naturalpetcare.co.uk Provides information on natural animal health (dogs cats, small animals, avian and horses) and also a shop where, in addition to food, you can find natural products to treat your pet's ailments and keep him healthy.

www.naturalpetchoice.com The health store for cats and dogs. There are ranges of dry and wet food, treats and chews, natural and hemp toys, grooming products and bio poop bags. They offer help and advice and you can read the blog.

www.scentaur.com A range of natural aromatherapy shampoos and grooming sprays for dogs.

Food

Many pet owners are concerned about the constituent ingredients of commercial pet food. It is quite one thing for the food to be made from the animal parts we humans do not choose to eat, but there are legitimate concerns regarding meat from carcasses considered not fit for human consumption and worse. **www.burns-pet-nutrition.co.uk/pet_food_labels.htm** gives you some insight into what can and cannot be gleaned from the label on the tin. If you don't want to risk it, try food from one of the following sources.

www.aminews.co.uk Made from natural ingredients and without 'slaughtered by-products' this brand of hypo-allergenic, vegetarian dog and cat food claims to reduces allergic reactions and keep your pets in top condition.

www.burns-pet-nutrition.co.uk Natural, holistic food for dogs, cats and rabbits with lots of advice on keeping healthy animals.

www.naturaldogfoodcompany.com Uses unadulterated wholesome, organic ingredients that the dog is supposed to eat and nothing else. They also offer an 'ask a holistic vet' service.

www.naturesmenu.co.uk High-quality natural dog and cat food made from 60 per cent raw meat that comes in a variety of flavours with an option of buying frozen. They also have baked biscuits for dogs. There is a good help and advice section.

www.organipets.co.uk They use organic and British originated meat (whenever possible) to make their dog and cat food. There is only one variety – chicken. Also sells dog treats.

www.pascoes.co.uk Dog, rabbit, guinea pig and hamster food all made from natural ingredients such as chicken, beef or fish, wholesome cereals and grains and vegetables.

www.veggiepets.com Moist and dry vegetarian food for dogs and cats including veg jerky chews and biscuits. They have biodegradable cat litter, natural dog accessories, herbal pet remedies and food for rabbits, guinea pigs and birds. There is information about vegetarian dogs and cats.

Vegetarian dogs?

There is good advice from the Vegetarian Society at **www.vegsoc.org/info/dogfood1.html**.

Natural health

www.natural-animal-health.co.uk This site is devoted to explaining many of the complementary veterinary therapies available for horses, dogs and other animals and pets. This includes chiropractors, homoeopathy, hydrotherapy, natural supplements and more. There are explanations of each therapy and how they work plus a list of vets offering such therapies. See also the earlier section on natural pet care.

Facts

- **There are 400 million dogs in the world.**

- **The average 11-kilogram dog will consume between 2.75 and 4 kilograms of chemical preservatives annually, if fed on commercial dog food preserved with chemical additives.**

Weddings

A white wedding or a green wedding? There's no need to compromise, just check out the following sites for advice on how to keep your eco conscience clean on the big day. We haven't broken the weddings down into all their component parts as the first few sites mentioned here are directories devoted to green wedding services with links on just about everything; however, you may also want to see the section on cut flowers on page 96.

www.allthingseco.co.uk This directory has a 'special' on weddings, which may provide some ideas to follow up using their links.

www.eco-friendlyweddings.co.uk A good place to visit for eco wedding ideas and wedding planning. What is really useful is the directory, which provides a comprehensive list of links.

www.greenandwhiteweddings.co.uk If you sign up to their free membership, they will provide downloadable wedding planning tools backed up with expert information and advice. There is a lot of good information on the site even if you don't sign up. Their particular interest is in finding perfect wedding locations.

www.greenunion.co.uk This 'eco friendly wedding website will help with everything you need to know about planning stylish, sustainable and ethical weddings and celebrations without compromising on quality or design'. Their wedding directory is a godsend for anyone planning a wedding and their planning advice is good too.

www.greenweddings.net An American site, but it might provide some inspiration.

www.ecomoon.co.uk Offers a range of services from complete wedding design and a full planning and co-ordination package, to a simple supplier search.

www.responsibletravel.com They have 329 ideas for honeymoons, so you should be able to find something wonderful. In the 'honeymoons' section there is a selection of green wedding packages located both in the UK and overseas – all guaranteed to be responsible, ecological and cultural.

Guilt free

An article from the *Independent* on how the big day doesn't have to literally cost the earth. It comes with links on how to find everything from a rickshaw to a ring.

www.independent.co.uk/environment/how-to-have-a-green-wedding-471576.html

---

After it's over, recycle

www.sellmyweddingdress.co.uk They will sell your wedding dress for you for a small fee, and, of course, you can buy your dress at the site (many dresses are new and unused).

Fact

● **The average wedding uses around 14.5 tons of carbon dioxide (as a comparator, the average is 12 tons per person per year).**

Funerals

Many of us want to pass out of life with the same ethical priorities that we strove towards in life. These sites offer the alternatives to a formal, traditional funeral. Maybe the best starting point is **www.ifishoulddie.co.uk** – not a green site per se but they have a good introduction to the concept of natural and woodland burials. This is an excellent site for the general overview of arranging a funeral and all attendant issues, both practical and emotional.

www.liferites.org Dedicated to the needs of those who hold no formal religious beliefs. On their site they run through a number of options, including DIY funerals and what you need to do to stay within the law. They will also provide a celebrant, should you need one. There are a few poems on the site and links.

www.naturaldeath.org.uk The website of the Association of Natural Burial Grounds has a listing of their members sites by county. The main aim of the site is to sell you their handbook, which, according to their account, will provide you with all the information that you need to arrange a greener funeral.

www.naturalendings.co.uk One of the most respected names in the businesses based in Manchester, but offering funeral arrangements to families throughout the northwest. Even if this is not your location, there is interesting information on the options open to you, which might help when you are specifying what you would like nearer to home. In other regions you could try **www.woodlandburials.co.uk** and **www.nativewoodland.co.uk**.

www.uk-funerals.co.uk Has information about all sorts of funerals including woodland burials, DIY funerals and burials at sea. There is also really helpful information on what to do initially after a death has occurred, a list of funeral directors (not green) by county and bereavement links.

Stop junk mail

Remove the name of the deceased from mailing lists by going to **www.the-bereavement-register.com**.

Coffins

www.daisycoffins.com Beautiful, natural coffins made from water hyacinth or banana leaves. Urns are available made from leaves or from wood.

www.eco-coffins.com For pine coffins made from managed, sustainable forests, using non-toxic glues and with no varnishes, oils, waxes, animal products, metal or plastic. The company has a Fairtrade ethos. The coffins can be ordered flat-packed.

www.ecocoffins.com Made from at least 90 per cent recycled cardboard, these coffins can be left natural, or come in a wood-grain effect or a colourfully designed alternative. There is the option to order plain white to customise with your own decoration; otherwise, they will custom one to your specifications.

www.ecopod.co.uk Uniquely designed coffins and urns made from naturally hardened 100 per cent recycled paper.

Freeze-drying (cryogenic freezing)

www.timesonline.co.uk/tol/news/uk/article577873.ece *The Times* ran an article about a novel Swedish solution to body disposal: freeze drying (not to be confused with cryopreservation). After being dipped in nitrogen the body crumbles into a powder, which decomposes in 6 to 12 months in a shallow grave.

http://en.wikipedia.org/wiki/Promession has the scientific explanation.

Online memorial sites

These sites provide an outlet for the bereaved to create a tribute to someone they loved. Once a memorial is created, other people can add their comments in a guestbook.

www.gonetoosoon.co.uk

www.muchloved.com

www.rememberlife.co.uk

Note: it is suggested that one of these sites may have unwittingly encouraged young people to consider taking their own lives, so there may be alterations in procedures for these sites on the horizon.

Donating to science

The ultimate gesture in recycling.

www.facingbereavement.co.uk/DonateBodyMedicalScience.html Answers some FAQs.

www.hta.gov.uk/about_hta/donating_a_body_to_medical_science. cfm How to go about donating your body to medical science. A dry read, but all the facts are here with links to the various university centres that are in need of donated bodies.

Facts

- Since the 1998 Environmental Protection Act, in order to comply with specified emissions, crematoria now use at least three times the amount of fuel (mainly gas) than they did prior to the act.

- The pollutant effects of burial on water supplies are largely unre-searched.

- It is suggested that around 11 per cent of the mercury contami-nation found in the North Sea fish originates from crematoria.

- In most soils, buried at six foot, a body takes around 75 years to decompose.

COOL HUNTING GREEN
DAVE EVANS

This, the second book in the *Cool Hunting* series, recognises that the hottest designs right now are those that promote a cleaner, greener and more beautiful planet. Designers all over the world are hailing 'green' as the new 'black' and taking up the call to reduce, reuse and repurpose existing resources in their products to inspire a greener world. The most ingenious designers know it can be done without sacrificing creativity, style or functionality. *Cool Hunting Green* is a fascinating collection of quirky, bold and unique products guaranteed to get you thinking, talking and maybe even acting in a more environmentally sensitive manner... without losing your cool! Each creation is presented with a web address and explanation, so it can be bought directly from the designer.

ISBN13: 978-1-904915-28-7   256pp   190 X 160mm   Paperback
Price: £12.99   Available Now

To buy this book phone Turnaround Publishers Services on 0208 8293002 quoting SB GWG and receive a special price of £9.99 with free p+p

www.southbankpublishing.com